DANNY ORLIS
AND THE
STRANGE FOREST FIRES

DANNY ORLIS
AND THE
STRANGE FOREST FIRES

By Bernard Palmer

Illustrated by

David Miles

Post Office Box 1099•Murfreesboro, Tennessee 37133

CONTENTS

Chapter One

DANNY'S NEW FRIENDS

DANNY ORLIS opened the heavy screen door and stepped out on the porch of his log cabin home at Angle Inlet, Minnesota. The night chill was still in the air. Little wisps of fog hung motionless over Pine Creek and the Lake of the Woods; here and there, birds began to chirp their merry melody. It was early in the morning, but already a thin curl of smoke spiraled from the chimney of the little cabin that stood fifty yards or so down stream. The tanned, muscular lad turned toward his dog Laddie lying quietly in the sun.

"Hi, Laddie, old fella," he said, reaching down and taking the big dog affectionately by the ear. "We're going to have to get along without you today. You know that we couldn't get close to a moose if you were along."

The dog pressed his head hard against Danny's knee and looked up pleadingly.

"Now, quit begging," he said. "You just can't go. That's all there is to it."

Danny tangled his fingers in his dog's long hair and squatted down beside him. It was hard leaving the old fellow behind, even for a day. Most of the time Laddie was with him, trotting contentedly along at his heels as he walked through the woods, or perching proudly on the deck of the *Scappoose,* his feet braced to keep him from tumbling into the water, as Danny fished or ran errands with his boat.

"You've got to stay at home today," Danny told Laddie again. "I don't want to hear any more out of you about it."

Just then Bonnie Blanshard came out on the porch of the other cabin and waved to him. "Hi, Danny," she called.

"Hi, Trixie."

Danny and Laddie went down the path toward her. She was small for her eleven years and straight as a willow sapling, with an impish little face that was usually smiling, and merry blue eyes that sparkled when she laughed. Her face and arms were almost as brown as Danny's and her blonde hair was done in pigtails. "To keep it out of the way," she had explained to Danny with a toss of her head.

"I didn't think you'd be up so early, Trixie," Danny said. "Something special going on?"

"Oh, we've been up for a long time," she answered, smiling. "At least I have. But if I hadn't gone in and wakened Tip, he'd still be in bed. The old sleepy head."

Just then her brother Morris, who was called Tip by his dad and almost everyone else, came out on the porch. "Just what are you telling about me, Trixie?" he asked.

"You know what a hard time I had getting you up. And after you made me promise to get you up so early this morning."

Tip laughed pleasantly. "You certainly spoiled a good dream," he said.

Tip came over and sat down on the step beside Danny. He was almost a foot taller than his sister, his shoulders were broad and strong, and his face was burned brown to the very roots of his flaxen hair. Danny had liked him a lot from the first time they were introduced a few days before.

"Are we all set to go on that expedition?" he asked. "It won't be long," Danny told him. "Can you be ready in about half an hour?"

"Sure thing. We've already had breakfast and I think Mom's packing our lunch. All I've got to do is get my camera and some more film and we'll be all set."

"Swell."

Danny's mother came to the kitchen door just then. "Danny!" she called, her clear, firm voice echoing through the woods. "Danny! Come to breakfast!"

Blackie, Danny's pet crow that he had taught to talk, flew down to the post beside the kitchen door. "Danny!" he called in a perfect imitation of Mrs. Orlis. "Danny! Danny! Danny!"

"Listen to that old crow," the young woodsman complained to the kids. "I never do know whether Mom is calling me or whether it's just Blackie." He put his hands to his mouth and whistled shrilly to let his mother know that he heard her. "I've got to be going, Tip,"

"Danny!" he called in a perfect imitation of Mrs. Orlis.

he said, "But I'll eat and be back as quick as I can."

"O.K.," Trixie put in. "We'll have everything ready by the time you get back."

When the Orlis family was seated about the breakfast table and Danny had asked the blessing, his dad turned to him. "Well, what have you got lined up for today, Son?"

"I promised Tip and Trixie Blanshard that I'd take them out in the boat and show them some of the Angle country. They have been wanting to go up Harrison Creek and see Cloud's old house and that little cemetery where the old Indian was buried."

"That's fine," Mr. Orlis said. "Those youngsters are terribly lonesome. I was going to suggest that you show them around a little."

"What about the garden, Danny?" his mother asked. "It's getting terribly weedy, and you know that you were going to hoe it for me today."

Mr. Orlis poured a little cream in his coffee and stirred it slowly. "I think maybe it wouldn't hurt the garden to wait for another day, Mother," he said. "I'll help Danny with it tonight when he gets back."

"You won't have to do that, Dad," Danny put in quickly. "We won't be gone so terribly long. Tip's got a new movie camera and he's been wanting to try to get some animal pictures, and Trixie wants to look around a little. We ought to be back in the middle of the afternoon."

"Well, anyway," his dad went on. "I think you ought to go with the kids this morning. You can do a lot more good befriending them than you could in the garden hoeing weeds."

"I guess you're right at that, Carl," Mrs. Orlis said. "Those poor youngsters need one friend up here." There was a long painful silence. Danny looked from his dad to his mother and back again.

"Dad," he said curiously, "why do the people around here have it in for Tip and Trixie and their parents, anyway? They seem like swell folks to me."

Mr. Orlis got up and poured himself another cup of coffee. "It's a long story, Danny," he replied slowly.

"It's a very long story. But mostly I guess it's because they just don't understand."

Danny looked at him curiously. He wanted to ask him more, but he could tell by his dad's tone that it was better to leave the subject closed. The clock in the living room struck six-thirty, and he began to eat his oatmeal hurriedly. The kids would be ready before he was.

While they were still sitting at the table Tom Rawlins, a neighbor from across the creek, came in.

"Would you like a cup of coffee, Tom?" Mr. Orlis asked.

The visitor dropped into a chair beside the kitchen range and crossed his legs. "Don't mind if I do," he said.

"Have you got your new trap line staked out yet, Tom?" Mr. Orlis asked after a moment or two.

"I don't reckon it's going to do any good to set up a new trap line in these parts," he snapped, setting his cup of coffee on the corner of the stove.

"I don't think it's as bad as all that," Mr. Orlis said evenly.

"It's as bad as all that, and worse!" He leaned forward and stared hard at Danny's dad. "It was a fine thing, you letting that Blanshard outfit into one of your cabins, Carl," he snapped. "I gave you credit for having more sense than that!"

"But the family has to have a place to live, Tom," Mr. Orlis replied.

"Let them live in a tent," Tom retorted bitterly, "or go back where they came from. We don't want the likes of them around here, anyway."

Danny's dad hesitated a moment or two, toying with his cup. "Yes," he said softly. "We could do that. We could refuse to have anything to do with them, and be mean to their children, and make their stay up here as miserable as could be." He paused and took a deep breath. "We could do a lot of things to them— but it wouldn't help any."

"It might not help," Tom snarled. "But it would show him how we all feel about that L & R Paper Company he works for coming up here and cutting off all the timber." His voice trembled with emotion as he went on. "You know what that's going to do, Carl Orlis? It will ruin this country! In two or three years we won't have any trees or game, either. There won't be a thing up here!"

"Now, Tom," Mr. Orlis cautioned calmly. "We don't know that they are fixing to do all that. Nobody has ever heard exactly what they are planning to do. And besides, treating Warren Blanshard and his family mean, just because we don't like what the L & R does, isn't the Christian way."

"You and your pious talk," Tom growled angrily. "You give me a pain in the stomach."

Danny's dad only grinned at him good-naturedly. So that was it, Danny thought as he sat there, listening. He felt the same, sickening pain in his stomach at the thought of what could easily happen.

Everyone knew that the L & R had been buying up the rights to cut pulp wood on all the land they could get their hands on. What if they were planning to move in a huge crew of men with power saws, and start cutting trees, wholesale, on the Angle? Blanshard must work for the L & R. What if that was what he and his family had come up for?

For an instant Danny's heart leaped to his throat and he felt his face flush. Why did Tip and Trixie and their folks come up here, anyway? He wasn't going to waste his time taking them out and showing them the country, or do anything else for them. He didn't care if no one else would have anything to do with them. It was no more than they deserved! And then Danny looked over at his dad. He knew that his dad loved the Angle country, too. He had left the city and had come up to the wild, beautiful lake country to make their home years before. Danny knew how deeply his dad must be hurt at the thought that the Angle might be ruined. And yet he treated the Blanshards as nicely as he did anybody else.

Danny gulped hard. Almost at once he was sorry for having gotten angry with Tip and Trixie. "O God," he prayed silently right there. "Help me to be nice to them. It isn't their fault, and besides, it isn't Christian to feel that way about anyone."

It wasn't long until breakfast was over; and, even though Tom Rawlins was there, Carl Orlis got down the Bible and handed it to Danny.

"I believe it's your turn to read for us, Son," he said.

Tom got noisily to his feet as soon as the Bible appeared. "I—I think I'll be going, Carl," he stammered.

When Danny had finished reading, he and his mother and dad took their turns praying together. It was wonderful to be able to sit around the table with their heads bowed and talk to God about their problems. Mr. Orlis prayed for quite a while about the Blanshard family. When it came Danny's turn he wanted to pray for Tip and Trixie, too. But he just couldn't pray about anything else excepting his beloved Angle. It made him weak and sick inside to think that something might happen to spoil the country that he loved so much. Finally they finished and for a moment or two sat about the table without speaking. Then Mrs. Orlis got to her feet and began to get the dishes cleared away.

Danny stood quickly, kissed his mother on the cheek and said, "I'll be back about four o'clock, Mom."

Chapter Two

AN OUTING WITH TIP AND TRIXIE

TIP AND TRIXIE BLANSHARD were already sitting in the boat. Tip had his camera in a case about his neck and was working with a light meter he used in taking pictures.

The instant Danny saw them there he turned to ice inside. To think that their dad had come up to help ruin the Angle! The very thought of it left him weak and cold and trembling. He'd like to order them out of the boat and go tell their folks that they'd have to move out of the cabin before dark. People like that didn't deserve anything better. They ought to have to live in a tent, or go back to Warroad or something.

They—he stopped abruptly. He couldn't blame Tip and Trixie for what the L & R was about to do. It wasn't their fault. Perhaps they felt as badly about it as the Angle folks did. Their dad might feel badly about it too, but there wouldn't be anything he could do about it. He only worked for the large paper mill. He didn't decide what they were going to do.

"O God," Danny prayed, "help me to be kind to them." He went out on the dock with his fishing tackle in one hand and a can of gasoline in the other.

"Well," he said, forcing a smile. "Are you all set?"

"All set?" Trixie echoed, her blue eyes sparkling. "I'll say we're all set. We've been waiting out here so long that Tip just about went to sleep again."

"Don't talk to me about going to sleep," Tip said good-naturedly. "The way you've been nodding I thought you were going to doze off and fall right out of the boat."

"I tried to hurry," Danny said, getting into the heavy, flat-bottomed boat and loosening the anchor rope that was tied around a post. "We would have to have company and make breakfast extra late this morning. I thought the guy was never going to leave."

"Was that your company that just left?" Tip asked.

"He certainly looked angry," Trixie added. "He came storming out of the house and got into his boat and rowed away without even speaking to us."

"That's the way Tom Rawlins is most of the time," Danny said, laughing. "It hurts him to speak to anybody."

He was going to say more, to tell them about what a sour old codger Tom really was, how he got mad at everything and everybody. And then he stopped. His dad always said that if a Christian couldn't find something good to say about somebody, he'd be much better off not to say anything at all.

"I'm glad he doesn't live on this side of the creek," Tip said.

Danny stopped a moment, checking mentally to

see that he had everything along that he needed. That was a trick his dad had taught him which had saved him a lot of trouble at different times.

"Well," he said, as he realized that everything they would be needing was aboard, "I guess we're ready to shove off."

"O.K.." Tip paddled the cumbersome boat out away from the dock and Danny pulled the starter rope. The outboard motor was old, but was tuned up like a finely jeweled watch. It leaped to life with a roar that broke the quiet of the morning and sang through the trees. The boat skimmed along the water.

"Say!" Trixie exclaimed, laughing as the wind whipped at her hair. "This is fun!"

"Wait until we get out on the lake," Danny said, "and we'll really open her up."

The boat lifted its prow high in the air as he opened the throttle and sent an ever widening v of waves rolling from one bank of the wide creek to the other. Bonnie and Morris sat there, smiles lifting the corners of their mouths as Danny slowed a little at the mouth of Pine Creek, and turned to the left toward Bear River and Harrison Creek.

"This is fun," Trixie kept saying over and over. "This is really fun."

Tip only grinned.

When they had been riding for ten or fifteen minutes they passed the schoolhouse and little sawmill set on the shore of the Lake of the Woods.

"What's that?" Tip asked.

"That's Tom Rawlins' sawmill," Danny said, "and the building next to it is our schoolhouse and church."

"Church?" Trixie echoed. "Do you have a church way up here?"

"Sure we do," Danny told her. "Of course, we don't have a regular minister. We don't have enough people for that yet, but we're figuring on one some day."

"If you don't have a preacher what's the use of having a church?" Tip asked.

"Oh, Dad, or one of the other Christian men does the speaking for services, and then we have Sunday school. I'll have to take you over there Sunday."

Trixie shook her head. "Not me," she said quickly. "I don't think I'd like it. Besides I like to play on Sunday morning."

"I don't think I care to go either," Tip added. "I went to church once, but it wasn't any fun."

"You mean you don't go to church?" Danny exclaimed as though he could scarcely believe it. "But how do you learn about Jesus?"

Trixie and Tip looked blankly at him. "What do you mean when you talk about learning about Jesus? I don't get it."

"Do you mean you haven't ever heard about Jesus?" Danny asked them. "You haven't heard how He came on earth hundreds of years ago and lived without sinning and died on the cross and was resurrected so that we could be saved?"

Tip fidgeted nervously.

"I—I'll tell you," Trixie offered after a moment or two. We haven't lived where there have been churches for the past six or eight years. And before that, I don't know. I guess we didn't get interested in going."

Danny reached back and cut the throttle so he could talk above the whine of the motor. "You'll have to go to Sunday school and church with me," he said firmly. "Why—" he stopped suddenly and sniffed the air.

"What's the matter?" Trixie asked. "What's wrong?"

He shut off the motor and for an instant or two sat there, looking first one direction and then another, sniffing the warm morning air.

"What is it?" Tip asked.

"Do—do you smell anything?" he asked tensely.

Tip and Trixie looked at Danny and then at one another. "No," the boy said. "I don't smell anything."

Danny sniffed again. "I do," he said firmly. "I smell smoke."

"Smoke?" Trixie repeated. "What's so strange about smelling smoke?"

"There isn't anyone living up here within five miles," he said, his voice trembling with excitement. "Smoke here can only mean one thing. A forest fire!"

"What's so terrible about that," Tip asked, "if nobody lives around here?"

"What's so terrible about a forest fire?" Danny

"Do you smell anything?"

echoed. "It's just about the worst thing that can happen in country like this. It kills off good timber and
cover for the game and birds. There isn't anything
worse than forest fires!"

Chapter Three

A "LITTLE" FOREST FIRE

"BUT I STILL CAN'T SEE what difference a little forest fire makes," Tip said, laughing. "It looks, to me, like there are a lot of trees up here. You'll never miss a few of them. Why not just let them burn?"

"Listen, fella," Danny said earnestly. He was still sniffing the air, still trying to catch a glimpse of a telltale wisp of smoke against the green of the forest. "If a forest fire ever gets going good," he went on, "it doesn't just take a few trees. It burns everything for miles and miles and miles. It kills the animals and birds and anything else that can't get out of its path. There isn't *anything* that the people who live up here on the Angle are more afraid of than a forest fire."

"A forest fire must be terrible," Trixie said. "All those poor little animals." She shuddered.

For a moment or two they sat there breathlessly, sniffing at the air like so many bird dogs and staring into the brilliant green forest that crowded down around the Lake of the Woods.

"I can smell it," Danny exclaimed. "But I can't quite locate it."

"I think you must be imagining something," Tip said. "I can't smell anything."

"I smell smoke, all right. I know it's smoke."

"If—if we don't locate it?" Trixie almost whispered. "What'll happen then?"

Danny's lips drew down to a thin, hard line and he sucked in his breath sharply. "We've got to," he said between clenched teeth. "We've just got to."

And then he took a step or two to one side and quietly began to pray. "O God, help us to find the fire. Help us to find it and put it out before it spreads across the Angle. Help us, before it's too late!"

Trixie and Tip looked strangely at one another, and then at Danny, as though they had never heard anyone pray before, but neither of them said anything.

A gull wheeled lazily above the motionless boat and from afar came the lonesome, mournful cry of a loon. But Danny and his friends scarcely noted them as they sat there, trying to locate some trace of the smoke.

"I think I smell it now," Tip said uncertainly, his voice charged with excitement. "It isn't so very strong, but I think I can smell it."

"I do too," Trixie put in.

"It must be over that way," Danny said, pointing in the general direction of Harrison Creek. "That's the way the wind's blowing."

"If we only had a pair of binoculars," Tip said under his breath.

"Binoculars!" Danny repeated. "Why didn't I think of them before! I've got Dad's field glasses in my tackle box."

The battered old tackle box that had once been his dad's was fished out from under the boat seat. Danny began to hammer on the lid. "Now isn't that something?" he muttered. "It won't come open. Hand me the pliers, will you, Trixie?"

"Here," Tip said, pushing past her as he crawled over the center seat. "Maybe I can help."

While the two of them fumbled frantically to open the stubborn box, Trixie stared into the trees as hard as she could. Once or twice she thought that she saw something faint and shadowy, but she couldn't be sure. And in an instant it faded away.

"This would happen at a time like this," Danny said desperately. "Most of the time you can't get the lid of this old box to latch shut if you tried. Now I can't get the thing open."

"Take the hammer to it," Tip suggested.

Just then Trixie squealed excitedly. "I see it!" she cried. "I see it! I see it!"

"Where?" the boys echoed in unison.

"Right over there!" she gasped. "Up in the mouth of the creek on the other side of that big pine tree. I know I saw it!"

Danny and Tip scanned the woods excitedly, but for a moment or two neither of them could see anything.

Then Danny cried, "I see it!" He dropped the

tackle box he had been holding on his knees and whirled to start the outboard motor. "Let's go!"

As the box hit on the floor it spilled open and the binoculars scooted under Trixie's feet. Danny jerked the starter rope and Trixie picked up the field glasses and adjusted them to her eyes.

"Here," Tip ordered, reaching for them. "Let me have those glasses. Let me take a look."

But she held tightly onto them. "I can see it plainly now," she said.

"How big is it?" Danny demanded as he shoved the throttle wide open and swerved to head up Harrison Creek.

"It isn't very big," she said, "but it does look like it's burning awfully fast!"

"It doesn't take long," he said under his breath. "In dry timber a fire can get out of control in ten or fifteen minutes."

"What're we going to do?" Tip asked excitedly.

"We'd better go back for help," Trixie put in. "We can't do anything about a fire like that ourselves, can we?"

"We've got to do what we can!" Danny said. "We don't have time to go and get any help." They were nearing the spot and he gasped when he saw how high the flames were leaping.

"But we've got to do something!" Tip exclaimed.

"The only thing we can do is turn to God in prayer," Danny said softly.

"Huh," Tip shrugged. "A lot of good that'll do."

But Danny didn't answer him. Instead he bowed his head and prayed hurriedly, "O Heavenly Father, You know all about this fire and how terribly serious it can be to the Angle and to all of us who live up here. You know that we're the only ones here to put it out. Please be with us, O God, and help us to get it put out before it gets away from us. Help us, Lord Jesus! In Thy precious name we ask!"

No one spoke for a moment after he finished. Then Trixie said helplessly, "But there isn't anything we can do to put it out, is there?"

Danny nodded grimly. "My dad told me about a thing he saw done one time to put out a small forest fire. I've never tried it, but it just might work. Here," he handed his hunting knife to Tip and took his scout hatchet out of its sheath. "Now, as soon as we hit shore, cut a bunch of those long poplar branches with a lot of leaves on them. Dip them into the lake and try to beat out the flames with them. It's our only chance!"

"What do you want me to do?" Trixie demanded.

"You'd better stay in the boat," he said quickly. "We don't want you to get hurt."

"Oh, no," she retorted determinedly. "You're not going to do that to me. I'm not going to stay behind in any boat when I can be helping too. I'm in on this as much as you two are. Tip, you've got to cut me some branches too. I'm going to be out there helping you!"

There was no time to argue with her. The fire had

They worked desperately, frantically—beating out the flames inch by inch—foot by foot.

already covered an area, some fifteen or twenty feet square and the flames were licking upwards, toward the tops of the trees. Evidently the fire had only been going a few minutes when they smelled the smoke, for it was still burning along the ground in the thick carpet of dead branches and pine needles and brush, and hadn't yet caught among the tops of the live trees.

"We've got a good chance with it!" Danny cried, reaching back to try and urge another ounce of speed out of the roaring motor. "If we can get it out before it catches the live trees afire we can get it out!" And if they didn't, he added to himself, it would go racing along from one tree top to another and nothing would be able to stop it! The boat touched shore and the three of them leaped out.

"O God," Danny breathed inwardly as he cut his branches and slammed the leafy tips into the lake to wet them. "O God, be with us and help us!" For some reason he was so slow—so terribly slow; every move, every action dragged like a snail while the fire spread faster and faster. Nevertheless, he was already flailing the flames by the time Tip had his branches cut and began to run down to the water's edge.

The dry pine needles and cones were burning like kerosene, popping and crackling and sending sparks high into the air. Trixie snatched up the hatchet, cut herself a handul of poplar branches and began to work beside the boys, beating frantically at the leaping yellow flames. Their faces and arms and hands were hot and dry. The smoke choked their breathing and bit into their eyes until the tears ran down their cheeks. Every now and then one of them stopped in a fit of coughing. But they didn't let up. Not even for an instant. They worked until their breath came in long sobbing gasps, until their backs throbbed with pain and the blisters stood out in the palms of their hands. They worked until they felt as though they couldn't move another step, desperately, frantically—beating out the flames inch by inch—foot by foot.

Chapter Four

AN OBSERVER

AT FIRST IT DIDN'T LOOK as though Danny and his friends were going to get the flames under control. A little gust of wind came up and sent the fire racing along the ground, a slender finger of disaster.

"Look!" Trixie cried, pointing toward it in terror. For the moment she was so frightened that she couldn't move.

But Danny swung his smoking branches violently and managed to beat it out before it reached a dead birch tree. Finally the blackened area began to grow and the dangerous yellow tongues of fire began to retreat stubbornly, inch by inch.

"We've got it now," Danny gritted between clenched teeth as he cut a new branch of poplar branches and wet them in the lake. "We've got it whipped now."

"I think so too," Tip gasped. And then they went to work again.

When at last they beat out the last flame, when they had stamped out the last spark and glowing ember, the three of them sank to the ground, exhausted. For several minutes they lay there drinking in the pure, clean air and resting their aching, weary bodies. Finally Trixie rolled over on one elbow and sat up, wiping her dirty, smoke-stained face with the back of her dirty hand.

"I thought we'd never get it out," she panted.

"Neither did I," Tip said, "but we did."

"With the help of the Lord Jesus," Danny added thankfully.

"The Lord?" Tip snorted in disgust. "I didn't see Him out there beating any flames out, did I? We were the ones who put out that fire. If there's going to be any credit handed out for doing it, we're the ones who deserve it."

Danny was sitting up now, wiping the dirt off his face with his handkerchief.

"Maybe you didn't see God out there beating out the flames, Tip," he said seriously, "but He was helping us just the same."

"How do you figure that?"

"Well, in the first place we had the strength to work until we got it out, didn't we?" the young woodsman asked. "I know I was so tired five minutes after we started that I didn't think we could ever get it out. We couldn't work that long on our own."

Tip said nothing.

"What would we do if the fire had had a head start on us of fifteen or twenty minutes more?" Danny went on. "What if it had gotten up in the tops of the trees so it could have swept along from one tree to another like forest fires so often do? We never could have put a fire like that out. What if the wind had come up even after we started to get it under control? What would have happened if I hadn't been close by when that little gust of wind started to spread the fire? or if Trixie hadn't happened to see it? What if—"

"Oh, well," Tip retorted, "if you're going to count things like that, maybe you could say He helped us. But it sounds more like plain ordinary luck to me."

"The trouble is," Danny said quietly, "that we want God to do everything for us when we pray, and just exactly the way we want it done. We would all have thought that it was a wonderful miracle if God had just wiped out the fire as we rode up in the boat." He turned on his side and sat up. "Sometimes it pleases God to do things just that way, but more often He wants us to do everything that we can to work things out. Then He'll help us with the things we can't do anything about. Just because we had to fight the fire ourselves doesn't mean that God didn't answer our prayer. I know that He did."

"I guess maybe you're right," Tip said reluctantly.

"And another thing," Danny went on. "We don't want to ever get the idea that all we have to do is sit down and fold our hands and let God take care of us. He wants to help us, but He doesn't want us to be a bunch of softies."

Tip rubbed the big blisters in his hands tenderly. Now that he had stopped working they began to hurt terribly. Once he started to speak, but stopped abruptly.

"You seem so sure of yourself, Danny," Trixie said,

"and what you believe."

"I am sure," he told her confidently. "We have the best authority in the world to prove it. We've got the Word of God, the Bible."

There was a long silence.

"What do you suppose started the fire, anyway?" Trixie asked abruptly.

"A cigarette," Tip put in quickly. "I read somewhere that cigarettes start more forest fires than anything else."

"I guess that's right about most fires in timber," Danny agreed, "but I don't think it's right about this one."

"Why not?" Trixie asked. "It would be awfully easy for a man to flip a cigarette over there on the bank, even if he was going along in a boat on the creek."

"You're right about that too," Danny said, "but I still don't think this fire started that way."

"Why not?" Trixie demanded once more.

"In the first place, the people who live around here who smoke know how dangerous it is to throw cigarettes around. They wouldn't think of doing anything like that any more than they would shoot a cow moose with a little calf."

"Maybe some outsider did it," Tip put in. "He could have come up on a fishing trip or something like that."

"There aren't any outsiders in these parts," Danny said. "That's one thing about the Angle. We usually know about it whenever anyone from the outside comes in. And there hasn't been anyone new for the last couple of weeks, excepting your dad. And we know that he hasn't been down this way today."

"Besides," Trixie said, "he doesn't smoke."

"Well, if it wasn't a cigarette, what did start it?" Tip asked him.

Danny got up and began to examine the charred ground. "I'm sure it wasn't a cigarette," he went on, "because those needles and pine cones are still a little damp on the outside from the rain we had a couple of days ago. They're as dry as ever on the inside, but it would take something mighty hot to get them to burning." He picked up some of the ashes and let them sift through his fingers slowly. "This stuff had to get awfully hot to char everything like this. Something terribly hot was used on them."

"Something terribly hot was used on these needles and pine cones."

"Like what?" Trixie asked.

"Gasoline," Danny whispered.

"You mean—" Tip's voice trailed away significantly.

"I mean I think it didn't start accidentally at all," he said tensely. "This fire was set!"

"Set?" Tip and Trixie echoed together.

"That's right," Danny repeated. "It wasn't a cigarette, and it wasn't lightning. We know that. There's only one thing left. Somebody wanted to start a forest fire up here!"

The youngsters' faces blanched white beneath the smoke and grime. "But why?" they asked, only mouthing the word. "Why would anyone want to do a thing like that?"

Danny shook his head. "I don't know—yet," he said.

They sat there staring at one another when suddenly Trixie grasped Danny by the arm and pointed across the creek. Her eyes were bugged wide and her mouth opened, but no sound came out.

"What's the matter?" Danny and Tip demanded at once. "What's wrong? What do you see?"

"I—I just happened to look up," she managed in a strangely choked voice, "and I saw someone. There's someone over there in the brush spying on us!"

"Are you sure?" Danny demanded harshly.

She nodded and pointed again. "He's right over there!"

Chapter Five

BOAT ADRIFT

DANNY AND TRIXIE AND TIP sat there tensely, not daring to breathe. Their eyes were riveted to the clump of brush Trixie was pointing to.

"I don't see anything," Danny said in a hoarse whisper. "I don't see anything at all over there except a lot of trees and brush and swamp grass."

"Neither do I," Tip said scornfully. "But she's got an imagination a mile wide. Are you sure that you're seeing something over there, Trixie?"

"Of course, I'm sure," she replied quickly. "He isn't there now, but he was a second ago. I just looked up and there he was, staring right at me!"

"It couldn't have been a deer or a bear you saw, could it?" Danny asked. "Sometimes they can fool a person."

"It wasn't anything like that at all, Danny," Trixie said seriously. "I saw him just as plainly as I'm seeing you. I just happened to look over that way and caught him peeking up over the brush looking at us."

The color drained from Tip's face and his eyes grew wider. "What do you suppose he's doing?" he asked. "What do you suppose he's watching us for?"

"He could have been the one who set that fire," Danny said softly. "We might have frightened him away before he got the fire going the way he wanted it."

His companions shuddered, and Tip scrambled to his feet. "We'd better get out of here," he said hurriedly.

"I'll bet he's terribly mad at us for coming along and putting it out."

"Maybe he's just waiting around to get even with us!" Tip put in suddenly, his heart racing at the thought. "Come on. Let's get out of here!"

"What did he look like?" Danny asked as they started to move as quietly as possible toward the boat.

"I don't know for sure," Trixie said. Her voice was still trembling, and Danny noticed that cold, nervous sweat beaded her forehead. "All I saw of him was the top of his head and his eyes. He had black, sort of bushy hair that looked as though it hadn't been combed for a week. And his eyes—" she paused and a shudder shook her. "It just felt like he was looking completely through me. And—and he was awfully brown."

"Do you suppose it was an Indian?" Tip asked looking about uneasily, as though he half expected to see an Indian brave dressed in warpaint come charging out of the woods with his tomahawk ready to get their scalps.

"More than likely it was some fellow who's been out in the sun a great deal," Danny said. "Almost everybody up here is burned dark by the sun in the summertime."

"Do you really suppose he's the one who set the fire?" Trixie asked again.

"Of course, it is!" Tip started to run, but Danny grasped him by the arm.

"Take it easy, Tip," he whispered. "If that fellow's still around we've got to be mighty careful." He got to his feet and slipped his hatchet into the sheath. "I'll lead the way, and you two follow."

With a prayer on his lips, he began to pick his way through the pine and basswood toward their boat. If the fellow who had been spying on them had been going to do them harm it looked as though he'd have done it by this time, Danny reasoned, as he inched slowly, carefully forward. Yet there was something strangely ominous about it all, something that squeezed his heart with fear and set his spine to tingling.

They had been only three or four hundred yards away from the boat, but Danny moved painstakingly, sliding each foot noiselessly along the ground. Tip and Trixie were on each side of him and a little to the rear. They were breathing heavily and moving on tiptoe in an effort to be quiet.

Perhaps, Danny thought to himself, the stranger was moving alongside of them, screened by the trees and laughing at their efforts to keep from making any noise. Perhaps he was waiting until they got down to the boat before he pounced upon them. Perhaps—just then Tip slapped at the mosquitoes that hovered about his head in a swarm and stepped backward onto a dead branch. In the hush of the afternoon it cracked like a rifle! Danny sucked in his breath sharply and signaled with his hand.

Trixie and Tip froze where they were standing! But it was too late! There was an instant of silence, then a loud curse and the sound of someone crashing headlong through the trees and muskeg upstream.

"The boat!" Danny cried excitedly. "Quick! Get to the boat!" For that was the direction the sound came from.

"Come on, Trixie!" Tip exclaimed, grasping his sister by the arm and half dragging her toward the place where the boat had been left.

Wildly they ran over fallen branches and through crackling brush down to the creek where the boat had been tied. Danny stopped short, staring at the empty bank.

"It's gone!" he almost sobbed. "Our boat's gone!"

The stub end of the anchor rope was still tied to the pine tree as he had left it, but it had been cut off neatly a foot or so from the tree. The stranger had cut the boat loose and pushed it adrift to leave them stranded!

"What're we going to do?" Trixie asked, her voice trembling. "What're we going to do now?"

"I don't know—" Danny started to say, but Tip broke in excitedly.

"There it is!" he shouted. "It's drifting toward the lake!" He pointed a hundred yards or so downstream to the heavy boat that was floating aimlessly toward

"What are we going to do?"

the open water of the Lake of the Woods. "But we'll never get it!"

"Oh, yes, we will!" Danny retorted. He peeled out of his shoes and jacket in a trice and dove into the sluggish creek. With long, powerful strokes he knifed through the water until he reached the drifting boat and scrambled into it. In a few minutes he was back to shore where Trixie and Tip were waiting for him.

"Boy!" Tip exclaimed as he crawled into the boat after Trixie and helped Danny shove off. "Let's get out of here before that fellow comes back!"

"That was really luck that we got here when we did," Trixie said. "If we had been another few minutes later, the boat might have drifted out of sight so far that we wouldn't have known where it was, or so far that you wouldn't have dared to swim to it."

Danny started the motor, and Tip put his oar back in the boat and took a deep breath of relief. "Yes, sir," he said. "We were really lucky. Lucky all the way through."

"I wouldn't say that it was luck, Tip," Danny answered as he turned along the weed bed and headed toward home. His heart was still hammering a loud tattoo against his ribs.

"If it wasn't luck I don't know what you'd call it," Tip countered.

"It certainly seemed like luck to me," Trixie put in. "I never was so frightened in my life. When I saw that our boat was gone, I thought we'd just be lost out in those woods for ever and ever."

"I guess I felt about the same way you did," the young woodsman said simply. "But it wasn't luck that we found the boat and got out of there. It was God answering our prayer."

Tip and Trixie looked at one another in bewilderment.

"You remember that I prayed out in the boat that God would help us to put out the fire," Danny went on, "and He did. Then I prayed all the while we were sneaking through the woods to get our boat. Sure, we had to work like everything, and I had to get all wet, but it wasn't luck that things worked out the way they did. It was God answering prayer."

For a couple of minutes they were silent. Danny turned the boat a little closer toward shore and adjusted the carburetor to get a little more speed out of his laboring motor.

"Do you think God really hears you when you pray to Him?" Trixie asked at last.

"Of course I do," Danny replied.

"Just like I hear you?"

"Just as you hear me," Danny said; "only better, really, because God hears when we think our prayers. That's something we can't do."

"Do you mean to tell me," Tip put in, "that if I'd pray to God that He'd hear and answer my prayer?"

Danny cut the motor a little so he wouldn't have to shout above it. "Now that depends," he answered. "God might answer your prayer sometime, and He might not. He doesn't promise to answer the prayers of those who haven't taken Christ as their Saviour."

Tip looked strangely at him. "I don't even know what you're talking about."

"The Bible tells us," Danny went on, "that when we confess our sins and take the Lord Jesus as our personal Saviour that we become the sons of God. God becomes our Father, and the promises He has made in the Bible become ours. He promises to answer the prayers of His children."

"I still don't get you."

"It's like this," Danny said, searching hard for words. "Supposing I'd come up to your dad and say, 'Father, give me the money to buy a new fishing rod.' What do you suppose he'd say?"

Trixie snickered a little at the thought. "He'd probably say that he has a hard enough time trying to buy his own kids the things he thinks they ought to have."

"Well," Danny continued, "that isn't exactly the way it is with God, for He doesn't have any trouble supplying the things we need. But He doesn't promise to hear and answer the prayers of those who aren't His children."

Tip picked up the oar nervously and laid it down again. "I still don't go in for that tripe," he muttered under his breath.

Chapter Six

A SEARCH

THE THREE YOUNGSTERS rode along in the boat for five or ten minutes without saying anything. Danny cast a quick look back toward Harrison Creek as though he half expected to see the telltale traces of smoke and flame again. Tip wiped the sweat off his forehead with the back of his grimy hand, and Trixie shuddered involuntarily.

"I wish we knew why that fellow was trying to set fire to the woods," she said. "Why do you suppose he'd do an awful thing like that, Danny?"

"I've been trying to figure that out," he said. "But it doesn't make sense to me. I don't see how it could possibly have gained him anything to start a forest fire way over there."

"Do you suppose he'll try it again?" Tip asked.

Danny bit his lip thoughtfully. "I'm certainly afraid that he will. I can't figure out why he'd want to start a fire, but he must have had a pretty good reason for trying to do it. A man just wouldn't do a thing like that unless he did."

Trixie's face blanched white. "Then you think—" her voice trailed away.

The young woodsman nodded. "If somebody doesn't stop him I just know that he'll try it again."

"If that's the case we'd better get the cops on him," Tip put in. "As soon as we get home I'm going to talk to Dad about it. He'll get the cops onto that fellow, and they'll clap him into jail before he has a chance to set another forest fire."

Danny smiled in spite of himself. "The cops?" he echoed. "Minnesota doesn't have any cops up here, Tip."

"What about the Canadian Mounties, then?"

"This happened in Minnesota," Danny explained, "so the Mounties wouldn't have had anything to do with it. But even if it had happened on the Canadian side of the border, the closest Mounties are in Kenora, sixty or seventy miles across the lake. And they've got so much to do that the chances are it would be a long while before they could get down here to look into something as little as this."

"But you said a forest fire isn't just a little thing," Trixie put in. "You said that it's terribly dangerous."

"Certainly it's dangerous," Danny replied. "But just the same, we don't have any real evidence that they could send a man to jail on. Besides, we don't know who the guy is, or what he looks like for certain."

"But we just can't stand around and do nothing," Trixie said heatedly. "If we don't catch him he'll start another fire when nobody's around and burn up the woods, and kill off the animals and birds and everything."

"Maybe we can do something," Danny said shortly.

"We can keep our eyes open for anything suspicious."

The girl bit her lower lip. "It frightens me just to think of it," she stammered.

Danny turned up into Pine Creek and headed for dock in front of his home. It might not make so much difference at that, he told himself almost angrily. A fire would be worse, of course, but if the L & R came in with pulp-cutting crews the timber and wild game would be gone soon, and the Angle would be ruined anyway. That feeling of fear welled in his heart again. How he wished that the paper company and the Blanshards had never heard of Angle Inlet!

But there was little time now for thinking about what was going to happen to the Angle. As the boat nosed in to the long, slender dock, Mrs. Blanshard came running out to meet them.

"Hi, Mom," they said almost at the same time.

She was a pretty woman a little younger than Danny's own mother, with blonde hair about the color of Trixie's, the same deep, flashing blue eyes, and the same quick smile.

"Oh, I'm so glad that you're back!" she said, the smile vanishing from her face.

"We were all right," Trixie assured her.

"Mrs. Orlis said that you would be," she went on, "but with you two gone, and Daddy gone, I was beginning to get awfully worried."

"Where did Dad go?" Tip asked quickly. "What happened to him?"

"I don't know that anything happened to him," his mother said. "But he told me that he was only going to be gone a little while, and it's been hours since he said he would be back."

"Where did he go?" Trixie asked as they walked along the dock to the bank of the creek.

"He borrowed one of Mr. Orlis' boats right after breakfast," Mrs. Blanshard continued, "and went over to International Island where he's building our cabin. He said that he wanted to check and see whether we had all the shingles that we needed, and he wanted to measure the windows which the lumber yard sent out." She took a deep breath. "He was supposed to have been back in an hour or so, and I haven't seen or heard anything of him since."

Danny eyed her carefully. She looked as though she might have been crying, and was so disturbed that she hadn't even noticed his own wet clothes, or Trixie and Tip's dirty, grime-smeared hands and faces.

"I wouldn't worry about him if I were you, Mrs. Blanshard," he said evenly. "There isn't much danger of getting lost between here and International Island, or anywhere up here on the Angle of the Lake of the Woods as long as you stay on the water. He probably just got busy on something or other and forgot to come home. Dad does that lots of times. Mom finally decided that it didn't do any good for her to worry about him."

"Yes," she countered quickly, "but there isn't anyone after your Dad like there is after—" Then she stopped quickly and clapped her hand over her mouth as though she had said something that she shouldn't have.

"Why?" Danny asked quickly, before he thought. "Is someone after Mr. Blanshard?"

Trixie's mother looked at him strangely for a moment or two. At first he thought she wasn't going to answer. Her face had taken on a grim, haggard look, and for the first time he noticed that her eyes were deeply circled. "In Mr. Blanshard's job," she said at last, "there is always someone who doesn't like him."

"Maybe we'd better get over there," Tip cut in. "Could you take us over to International Island, Danny?"

"Sure thing." He started toward the gas barrel which they had on blocks to the left of the dock. "I'll fill up old Betsy, go tell Mom where I'm going; and we'll be over there in fifteen minutes."

"Would you go?" Mrs. Blanshard echoed gratefully. "I suppose everything is all right, but I'd feel a lot better if you could run over and be sure."

Danny had Trixie run into the house and help his mother make them some more sandwiches while he and Tip filled the motor with gasoline.

"Well," he said when she came back. "I guess we're ready to go."

Mrs. Blanshard looked at Danny appealingly. "You will be careful," she said uncertainly. "Won't you, Danny?"

He smiled up at her. "You won't need to worry about us," he said.

As they started to shove off from the dock Laddie came running down and jumped heavily into the boat, almost landing in Trixie's lap.

"What do you think you're doing, old man?" Danny said to him. "Who told you that you could go along with us?"

Trixie put her arm about the neck of the big shepherd dog. "He can go along, can't he?" she asked.

"I guess so." Danny laughed. "It looks as though we aren't going to be able to get away without him. He usually goes every place I go."

It had been after six o'clock when Danny and the other two had come into the dock. Now the shadows were beginning to lengthen across the water, and the sun was hidden behind a fringe of clouds. The faithful old motor was still purring smoothly.

"How far is it to International Island?" Trixie asked for the fifth time in as many minutes.

"Not so far," Danny told her. "We'll be there in another five minutes or so."

"What do you suppose could have happened to Dad?" she asked.

"Nothing, probably," Danny told her. "When we get over there we'll likely find him working so hard on the cabin that he's forgotten what time it is."

"Yeh," Tip agreed. "That's probably what we'll find." But his voice didn't sound as though he completely believed it himself.

Danny docked the boat in a little cove on the north-

"S-s-s-st," Danny said hoarsely.

western corner of the island that straddled the American-Canadian boundary, and they began to walk quickly up the narrow, winding path toward the place where Mr. Blanshard was building a cabin for himself and his family.

By this time it was dark enough for Danny to use his flashlight. As they walked along behind him in single file Trixie said, "Well, in a couple of minutes we'll find Daddy."

"He'll probably be wondering what all the fuss is about," Tip told her.

At that very instant they heard a low, unnatural cry come from somewhere up ahead. "S-s-s-st," Danny said hoarsely.

"Help!" they heard again.

"Did you hear that?" Trixie asked softly.

Chapter Seven

THE RESCUE

DANNY ORLIS sucked in his breath sharply. Icy fingers of fear squeezed at his heart, and the color drained from his face. What was it that Mrs. Blanshard had said about someone being out to "get" the kids' dad? What was it that she had been afraid of?

The sound came again, weak and far away.

"Did you hear anything?" Tip demanded hoarsely. "Did you?"

Danny nodded, his lips set in a thin, hard line.

For a brief instant they stood there looking at one another. Trixie's lips were trembling, and her cheeks were an ashen white. She started to speak, then stopped suddenly.

It came again—a low, agonizing moan from somewhere just ahead. It sounded almost like the cry of an injured animal, a sound which Danny had often heard in the woods, yet it had a human quality about it.

"W-w-what is it?" Trixie asked in a hoarse whisper. "What is it?"

But Danny didn't answer her. Instead he went scrambling up the steep, rocky path at top speed.

"Come on!" he called. "Hurry!" There wasn't a moment to lose. Whoever was up there could be hurt and hurt badly!

Danny had started up the trail three steps ahead of the others, but it was Tip who reached the half-finished cabin first. With a sudden burst of speed, he shot past Danny and rushed into the clearing. There, for a split second, he stopped short, fear and surprise rooting him to the ground. At the foot of a ladder propped against the half-finished cabin, his dad was sprawled motionless.

"Dad!" he cried. He ran forward and dropped quickly to the ground beside his father. "Dad! Dad! What happened? What's the matter?"

The man groaned again and tried desperately to move. By that time Danny and Trixie had reached the place where he lay. Trixie choked back a sob, and she and Danny knelt beside Mr. Blanshard.

Quickly Danny examined the injured man for broken bones and felt his burning forehead. More than once he had been with his father in the woods when someone in the party got hurt, sometimes seriously. He knew what to do.

Mr. Blanshard had been hurt several hours before, because fever had already set in. His lean, muscular face was creased and twisted with pain, and his pulse was racing and uneven.

"What happened, Dad?" Trixie and Tip were exclaiming almost together. "What's wrong? Are you badly hurt? Are you—"

"My head," he groaned. "My head." Then he closed his eyes and seemed to drift back into unconsciousness again.

Danny pushed Trixie gently aside and turned her father's head carefully. What he saw caused him to gasp. The back of Mr. Blanshard's head was wet and sticky with blood that had oozed from the long, ugly gash. He was badly hurt.

Trixie's lips quivered as she looked at it, but she bit them savagely and didn't cry.

"We'd better get him home as quickly as we can!" Danny said, struggling to keep his voice calm. "If Mom can't fix him up we'll have to get him to a doctor, pronto."

"But how'll we ever get him down to the boat?" Trixie asked.

Tip got to his feet. "You and I will have to carry him, Danny."

"And you, Trixie," Danny said, "get down to the boat and fix a place to lay him. Hurry."

She was gone in a flash.

Mr. Blanshard was by no means a small man, and when the boys finally got him down to the boat their breath was coming in long sobs and their arms and shoulders were trembling. Trixie helped them lay him as comfortably as possible in the prow of the boat and shove the craft into the water.

"Now," Danny gasped as the big motor leaped to life with a roar. "We'll have him back to our cabin in

"You and I will have to carry him, Danny."

no time!" He spoke confidently, but he knew, even better than his companions, how badly their father was hurt. The accident had happened some hours earlier and he had lain there, suffering from shock and loss of blood.

For several minutes they rode into the growing darkness without speaking. Then Tip turned to Danny. "Dad's badly hurt, isn't he?" he asked.

Danny nodded solemnly. "I don't know how serious it is," he said, "but I do know that he's lost quite a bit of blood. But Mother and Dad will know for sure. They've seen a lot of accidents up here in the woods."

Trixie had taken off her coat and was pulling it up around her father's shoulders. "Give me your coats," she said to Tip and Danny. "Dad's shivering with the cold."

When they had done so Tip leaned forward and said, softly, "Danny, would you pray for Dad?"

"I have been praying for him, Tip," Danny answered. "I've been praying for him ever since we first found him back there."

"I know," Tip replied. "But would you pray for him again? Out loud, I mean. I—I've been trying to pray, but I keep remembering what you said about God not promising to hear and answer the prayers of—of those who aren't His children." Tip choked up and for a minute or two he could not go on. "Won't you pray for him, Danny?"

"Sure, I will." Without bowing his head or closing his eyes—for he was running the motor at top speed and dare not lose a second, Danny began to pray. "O heavenly Father, You know all things. You know how this accident happened to Mr. Blanshard and how badly he's hurt. You knew about it even before we found him. We want to thank You for guiding us to him and helping us to get him down to the boat. We want to thank You that we found him tonight instead of tomorrow morning. With the fever and mosquitoes and black flies tomorrow might have been too late.

"Now, O Lord, we pray that You would help us to get him to someone who can take care of this wound on his head, that You would just watch over him and care for him with Your healing hand."

For a moment or two Danny paused; Trixie and Tip

were sitting with their heads bowed and their eyes closed. "But, O God, You know that there's something more important than healing Mr. Blanshard's body. If he hasn't found Thee as his personal Saviour, O Lord, just guide him into a saving knowledge of Thee. Lead him and Trixie and Tip to Thee, Lord Jesus. In Thy precious name we pray. Amen."

There were tears standing full in Trixie's eyes, but neither she nor Tip spoke until the boat nosed into the dock and Danny called, "Dad! Dad! Come here, quick!"

Carl Orlis came running out onto the dock. "What's wrong, Son?" he asked. "What's the matter?" And then he saw the injured man lying in the bottom of the boat. "Here," he said. "Let me get him into the house." He picked up Mr. Blanshard easily and carried him into the bedroom of the Orlis' cabin.

Mrs. Blanshard saw them and came hurrying over, her face white and drawn with fear. "I knew they'd do it," she said softly. "I knew they would."

Carl Orlis had his big first-aid kit out and had begun to swiftly and expertly wash out the wound with disinfectant and treat Mr. Blanshard for shock.

The injured man groaned a little and opened his eyes. A weak little smile flitted across his lips as he saw Mrs. Blanshard standing at the foot of the bed.

"How is he?" she asked, her lips scarcely forming the words. "How is he, Mr. Orlis?"

"I think he's going to be all right," Danny's dad said at last. "He might have a little concussion. We'll have to watch him closely for that, but I'm quite sure that his skull isn't fractured. And he seems to be gaining consciousness now."

"Thank God," Mrs. Orlis breathed reverently.

"What he needs right now is plenty of rest." With that Mr. Orlis shooed everybody out of the bedroom except Mrs. Blanshard who sat there holding her husband's hand.

Chapter Eight

A VEILED WARNING

IT WAS LATER THAN USUAL when Danny got to bed that night, and he was exhausted, but try as he would he could not get to sleep. The strange fire that had almost gotten away from them, the evil-looking man Trixie had seen staring at them through the brush, the man who had set their boat adrift, and finding Mr. Blanshard badly hurt—all these thoughts kept running through his mind.

It could have been that those things had just happened, that there wasn't any special meaning to the incidents. And yet he couldn't forget the terror in Mrs. Blanshard's face when she saw that her husband was injured. He could never forget her voice, "I knew they'd get him!" What did it mean? What did Mr. Blanshard's accident mean, and the forest fire? Those questions kept revolving, without answer, in his mind.

Finally he dropped off to sleep, but at the first sound in the room below he awakened and got up.

He came downstairs just as Tip and Trixie hurried into the house.

"Hi," he said to them.

"How's Daddy?" they asked quickly.

"Why don't you go in and see him?" Mrs. Orlis said, smiling. "I think he feels a great deal better. He's been asking for the three of you."

"Hi, kids," Mr. Blanshard said when they entered the room. He managed a crooked little grin.

"How do you feel, Daddy?" Trixie asked anxiously.

"I've got a whale of a headache," he told her, "but aside from that I feel pretty good."

"We were so worried about you last night," she went on. "I thought maybe—" her voice trailed away weakly.

He raised up on one elbow and took a drink of water. "I guess it was lucky for me that you kids came along when you did."

"What happened, Mr. Blanshard?" Danny asked.

The smile left his face. "I don't just know for sure," he said. "I started to climb up the ladder and fell. I must have hit my head on the edge of a sawhorse."

Relief came across Danny's face. So there wasn't anything mysterious about his getting hurt after all.

"I wanted to talk with you three alone," he said. For an instant he looked past Danny into the other room, as though trying to see whether anyone else was in that part of the house. Then he whispered, "Close the door, Tip."

The boy went to close the door, and then the three of them crowded closely about his bed.

"I can't tell you everything right now," he whispered. "But I think I'm going to have to call upon you kids for help. At least until I can get back on my feet again. Can I count on you?"

Trixie and Tip nodded quickly.

"How about you, Danny?" Mr. Blanshard asked, looking squarely at him.

"I—I suppose so," Danny said, his cheeks flushing hot. What had he promised to do—help Mr. Blanshard bring in the pulp crews to the Angle and spoil the forests and drive out the game? Had he promised to help destroy the little paradise in which they lived?

If Mr. Blanshard noticed his hesitancy he didn't mention it. Instead he said, "Mr. Orlis said he was going to send you kids in to Penasse this morning to get some supplies. While you're gone I would like to have you do something for me."

"Okay," Danny and Tip told him.

"Don't say anything to anybody about it," he went on, lowering his voice. "But on the way I'd like to have you stop by International Island and pick up that ladder I fell off of and bring it here to me."

"The ladder?" Trixie echoed. "What are you going to do with a ladder? You can't even get out of bed for three or four days, let alone climb a ladder. And a broken one at that!"

"You never mind what I plan to do with the ladder, young lady." Her dad smiled. "You just get it and bring it to me. And don't say anything to anyone about it for now, not even your folks, Danny."

When breakfast and the morning devotions were over, Mr. Blanshard called Danny into his room again. This time he got him alone and had him shut the door.

"Danny," he began slowly. "I want to thank you for what you did for me last night. I really appreciated it."

"That was all right," Danny said self-consciously. "Going over there wasn't anything. Mrs. Blanshard is the one who got disturbed about your not coming home when she thought you should have. She's the one who asked us to go over and look for you."

"That isn't what I mean," Mr. Blanshard continued. "I must have been unconscious when you boys were carrying me and when we were in the boat headed for home, but I wasn't unconscious when Tip asked you to pray for me. That's what I want to thank you for."

Danny sat there silently for a moment or two. "We always make a practice of praying about the things that trouble us," he said at last. "I guess it almost comes naturally."

"You know," the man went on seriously, "I haven't heard anyone pray for me since I was a boy younger than you are and used to hear my mother pray for me and my brothers and sisters that way. I guess I didn't appreciate it then. I certainly did everything I could to keep her prayers for me from being answered." He closed his eyes for a moment or two. "All a fellow has to do is start to slip and lose interest in spiritual things," he said more to himself than Danny, "and he can drift awfully far from God."

"Yes," Danny told him, "but it's just as easy to come back to Him. God's always waiting for you."

"Yes," Mr. Blanshard almost whispered, "I suppose He is. I suppose He is."

There was another long, painful silence. "Wouldn't you like to do that now?" Danny asked. "Wouldn't you like to get back in fellowship with the Lord Jesus?"

"I don't know." The man's voice was harsh, and for a moment his eyes grew hard and cold. Then he softened and said, "Danny, would you hand me that Bible on the dresser and then leave me alone for a while?"

Danny started to speak, then stopped and handed the Bible to Mr. Blanshard. With a prayer in his heart he tiptoed out of the sick room and carefully closed the door. His dad was waiting for him in the living room.

"I was just coming in after you," Carl Orlis said. "I want you to go to Penasse and meet the mail boat. The captain said he would like to stop off there today if we could come after the mail for Angle Inlet. He's bringing out some things for us from town too."

"Sure thing, Dad," Danny told him.

"And, Danny," Mr. Orlis went on. "Keep your eyes open today. This thing that's happened to Mr. Blanshard has got me worried. I don't like it at all."

"What do you mean?" Danny asked him.

Mr Orlis ran his fingers through his graying hair. "I just don't know," he said. "It looks like an accident, all right, but I'm not at all convinced that it is."

By the time Danny had the motor greased and filled with oil, Trixie and Tip were ready to go.

"What do you suppose Dad wants with that ladder?" Tip asked as soon as they were in the boat and headed toward Penasse. "I don't remember much about it, but it looked like any ordinary old ladder to me. I can't see why he'd want us to make a special effort to stop by the island and get it."

"You don't suppose he's got something hidden in it, do you?" Trixie asked eagerly. "You don't suppose he hollowed out one of the rungs or something and has some secret papers hidden in it?"

"Of course, he didn't," Tip retorted. "Why would Dad be doing a thing like that?"

"He acted very mysterious," she went on.

Danny did not answer. He had another idea for the reason that Mr. Blanshard wanted the ladder, but he didn't care to say anything about it to Tip and Trixie right then.

"Why do you suppose Dad wants us to help him?" Tip asked. "And what do you figure he's got for us to do?"

"Boy, I don't know," Danny replied. "But he did sound as though it was something terribly important."

By the time they reached Penasse the mail boat had already arrived, and a dozen or so Indians and white settlers had gathered at the little backwoods' post office and store to get their mail.

Some of them Danny knew. There was Peter Olson from Potts' Musky Camp at Monument Bay, and a couple of Indians who guided out at Frolander's resort, and two or three woodsmen who had small places along the shores of the Angle. But there were two or three others Danny had never seen before. They were tall, somber-looking men with piercing dark eyes and straight black hair. The sin of their lives was written across their dark, swarthy faces, and they cursed frequently when they talked. They gave Danny a strange, uneasy feeling.

"I'll take care of you in just a minute, Danny," the Skipper called when he saw him. "It was certainly good of you to come over here so we didn't have to go on in to Angle Inlet today. There's a mechanic staying here at Penasse who's going to help me do some work on the boat."

"I was glad to come over, Cap," Danny said.

The instant the Skipper mentioned Angle Inlet, one of the strangers straightened suddenly and came over to where Danny was standing.

"You come from Angle Inlet?" he asked. "No?"

"That's right," Danny said, striving hard to be nice to him. "I live over there with my folks."

"I see." The stranger stroked his scarred chin and eyed Danny darkly. "You have excitement over there yesterday. Isn't that right? Big excitement."

"Excitement?" Danny tried to sound casual. "We always have excitement over there."

"The man with the broken head. Is he all right now?" He grinned crookedly as he saw Danny start at the mention of Mr. Blanshard. "It was so bad he have

"You tell that one for me that he better be careful," accident. So very bad. He must watch himself, that one. The next time he not be so lucky."

The young woodsman turned quickly, his heart hammering a wild tattoo. "Is my mail ready, Skipper?" he asked.

The stranger touched Danny on the arm. "You tell that one for me that he better be careful," he said. "You tell him he shouldn't go up on ladders. Maybe he shouldn't even go back and try to finish his cabin. Very dangerous for man to try to build cabin when he not even able to stand on ladder without falling."

Danny didn't answer him. Instead he turned to Tip and Trixie. "Come on," he said, "we've got to get going."

"Why?" Tip asked. "What's the hurry?"

"We've just got to get going," Danny repeated insistently, hurrying them down to the dock. When they were out of earshot of the stranger he said softly, "Didn't you notice that fellow who was talking to me? He was trying to pump me about your dad."

"Do you suppose he—"

"I don't know," Danny cut in. "But let's get out of here, fast."

As Danny started the motor the tall, swarthy stranger came striding out of the post office and headed for the dock where his boat and motor were tied.

"Do you suppose he's coming after us?" Tip asked excitedly.

Danny shook his head.

Chapter Nine

MR. BLANSHARD "GETS RIGHT" WITH GOD

"I THINK that fellow's going to try to follow us!" Trixie whispered excitedly. "He came out of the post office right after we did and now he's getting into his boat and starting the motor! He is following us, Danny!"

Tip leaned forward tensely, staring at the stranger in the other boat. "That's right, Danny!" he exclaimed after a moment or two. "He's heading right this way! He is going to follow us. What can we do?"

Danny shook his head and laid a warning finger across his lips. "S-s-sh," he whispered. "Remember how our voices carry over water. We won't want him to hear us. If he is going to follow us we don't want him to catch on that we know it."

"But what are we going to do?" Trixie asked hoarsely.

"We'll head straight for home," Danny said to them, cutting the throttle to half speed. "We'll act just as though we only came for the mail and the things Dad had the Skipper pick up for him and are heading back.

If he is after us I've got a hunch he just wants to find out where we are going and what we're doing."

A huge floating island of muskeg loomed up in their path, and he swerved sharply to avoid it. As he did so he took a quick glance back. "The guy's breaking out his fishing gear now," he said. "He acts like he's going to troll."

Tip sighed deeply. "Boy," he said, "I was certainly scared for a minute or two. I was positive that he was following us."

"Don't be too sure that he isn't," Danny warned. "He can still keep an eye on us. The fact is, he might be pretending to fish just to throw us off guard."

"That's right," Tip agreed. "But how are we going to find out for sure?"

Danny thought a moment. "Whatever we do," he said, "we don't want to let him know that we're watching him." He reached over and opened the tackle box to make sure that the field glasses were there. "Trixie," he ordered, "get those field glasses out of the tackle box and lie down in the bottom of the boat so you can watch him without being seen."

The man in the other boat appeared to be paying no attention at all to them. He cut his motor to trolling speed and was angling along the shore following the weed beds. Trixie gave the boys a move-by-move account of what he was doing.

"Now he's putting his fishing rod away," she whispered when they were about a mile away from him. "'And now he's starting to watch us through a pair of field glasses!"

"Oh, boy!" Tip exclaimed.

"That's just what I thought," Danny said. "Be sure and stay down, Trixie, so he doesn't see that we're watching him."

For several minutes Danny kept straight on the course toward home, until they passed the tip of Massacre Island. Then he began to edge northward until the island lay between them and Penasse.

"Can you see him now?" Danny asked Trixie at last.

"Not any more," she said. "The trees are in the way."

"Good!" he exclaimed. "That's just what I've been waiting for. Now we're going to fool that fellow." There were a dozen islands or so stretching almost from shore to shore, and Danny began to weave among them. With the motor at top speed, he headed north, doubled back to the south, circled east around a long, curved island and then turned west toward International Island. Every now and then he cut the throttle to listen for the sound of the stranger's motor boat. At first they heard it plainly, but after fifteen or twenty minutes the sound of it had completely disappeared.

"He's gone," Tip said hopefully. "At least I don't hear his motor any longer."

"He's given up," Danny laughed. "He knows that he can never catch us now. With the head start we've got and all these islands to dodge among he'd have to have an airplane to find us."

Tip and Trixie both sighed with relief. "I just don't know what I'd have done if he had caught us," she said. "He was one of the awfullest-looking men I ever saw."

"We gave him the slip, all right," Danny said. "I don't think he'll be bothering us again today."

At International Island they pulled the boat up under the low, overhanging branches of a tree, and Danny took time to camouflage it carefully. "We don't want to take a chance on losing our boat again today," he said.

"I thought you said we had ditched that fellow," Tip put in.

"Just a precaution."

Even before they reached the clearing Danny could smell the strong, pungent odor of burning wood and could see faint wisps of gray smoke against the clear blue sky, but he didn't say anything to either Tip or Trixie, and they didn't notice it. He started to walk a little faster. Perhaps—perhaps—and then they came into the clearing.

"Look!" Trixie cried in dismay. "Look at our cabin!"

Tip sucked in his breath sharply. All that was left of their almost completed cabin home was a few smoldering embers.

"What do you know!" Danny exclaimed. A sick feeling welled in Danny's heart. Somebody was out to get Mr. Blanshard after all.

The people who lived on the Angle were angry that

Mr. Blanshard and his family had moved up to the Lake of the Woods. They were angry and concerned over the fact that the L & R Paper Company was about to start to cut pulp wood on a scale that might soon denude their beautiful land of timber. But it didn't sound like them to burn down the Blanshard cabin.

"Who would do a thing like this, Danny?" Tip asked, bewildered. "Who would hate us so much that they'd burn our home?"

"Maybe it wasn't set fire," Trixie put in. "Maybe it just happened to burn."

The two of them looked at Danny but he said nothing for a moment or two. Cabins didn't "happen" to burn unless they were struck by lightning, or a stove or a cigarette set fire to them.

"I'm afraid it didn't just happen to burn, Trixie," he said at last. But the regular people on the Angle couldn't have set fire to the cabin. They just wouldn't. And besides, the stranger didn't fit into that picture. Why should he care what happened to the Angle and its forest and its game? There was something else here. Something that he didn't understand at all!

"Look!" Tip cried, pointing toward the smoking ruins. "There's the ladder Dad fell off!"

Three or four feet of the base had been burned, but the top half was still intact. Danny leaped forward and jerked it out of the fire.

"Oh, part of it burned!" Trixie said, looking at it. "Maybe the part Daddy wanted is gone!"

For two or three minutes Danny and Tip examined

*"Somebody wanted that ladder to break
with your dad on it,"*

the ladder without speaking. It had been standing against the building when they had been there the night before, but whoever set the cabin afire had accidentally knocked it down. Danny picked up the unburned section and stood it up. Tip ran his finger along one of the top rungs.

"Did you notice this, Danny?" he asked, indicating the cut of a saw on the rung which had been carefully filled with darkened beeswax.

Danny nodded. The top five or six rungs had been sawed in half and the cuts filled.

"Somebody wanted that ladder to break with your dad," Danny said at last.

"But who?"

Tip's eyes narrowed. "It must be the same person who burned our cabin," he told Trixie.

An hour later, when the boys and Trixie opened the door to Mr. Blanshard's bedroom he was lying there with his eyes closed and the open Bible in his lap. He opened his eyes quickly and smiled at them.

"I've been reading all morning," he said, "until my eyes got so tired I shut them for a couple of minutes. I guess I just fell asleep." He closed the Bible carefully and laid it on the table beside the bed.

The kids stood there staring at him until he reached out slowly and grasped Tip by one finger. "What's the matter, young fellow?" he asked. "Are you so surprised to see that I'm lying here reading the Bible?"

"I don't know, Dad," Tip said uncertainly. "It's just that I—" His voice dwindled away.

"Were you going to say that it startled you because you've never seen me reading the Bible before?" his dad asked.

"I guess so."

"I don't blame you for being surprised. I'm rather surprised at myself." He was quiet for a minute or more. "As far as the Lord Jesus Christ is concerned I've been asleep for a long while. But Danny, here, woke me up last night when he prayed for me and then when he talked with Him this morning. I've been spending the time since then in reading and praying. I've gotten 'right' with God."

"That's wonderful," Danny put in softly.

"A fellow never really knows how wonderful it actually is until he tries it for himself," Mr. Blanshard concluded.

Tip and Trixie were still silent with surprise at what had happened.

"Now tell me," their dad said, changing the subject abruptly. "Did you find the ladder?"

He didn't seem to be surprised to learn that he had fallen because the rungs on the ladder had been cut almost through, nor that their beautiful new cabin, which he had been working so hard on, had been burned. "It was about what I had expected," he said. "But please don't say anything to your mother about it unless she asks you. She's got enough to worry about as it is, and there isn't a thing that she, nor any of us, can do about the cabin now except to build it again."

"You aren't going to build another cabin over there, are you?" Trixie asked, her lips trembling uncertainly.

"Of course, I am, Trixie," he said. "You want to remember that I came up here to do a job. I've got to build a cabin for us."

The way he spoke struck fear to the depths of Danny's heart. Mr. Blanshard was determined to ruin the beautiful Angle country!

Chapter Ten

A VISIT TO RICK THUNDERBIRD

NOT UNTIL AFTER he had gone to bed did Danny think to tell Mr. Blanshard about the strange Indian who had talked to him at Penasse. He got up quietly and tiptoed down the stairs, but the bedroom door was closed and the lights were all out. He stood there for a moment or two, debating whether to waken Mr. Blanshard, then he turned quietly and tiptoed up to bed.

He got up early the next morning and went down to the injured man's room. Tip and Trixie were already there.

"The kids were just telling me about the strange Indian who talked to you about me yesterday," Mr. Blanshard said when Danny came in. "I'm certainly glad that you were wise enough to give him the slip before you stopped at International Island to pick up that ladder. If he'd caught you snooping around there's no telling what he might have done to you."

"Who is he, anyway?" Danny blurted. "There's so much going on around here that I don't know anything about that. I'm in a whirl most of the time. Who is this fellow? And what is he trying to do?"

"I wish I knew all the answers to what's going on here, Danny," Tip's dad said, smiling. "There are a good many things taking place which I don't understand myself."

Tip eyed his father quizzically. "Why can't you tell us what you do know, Dad?" he asked.

"Yes, Daddy," Trixie put in. "It's just like trying to work a jigsaw puzzle with most of the pieces missing."

Mr. Blanshard was quiet for a long while. "I'd like to tell you what I know," he said. "But to be honest with you I haven't decided whether I dare to take you into my confidence or not. I'd never forgive myself if I let you into something that would cause you to get hurt."

"But we won't get hurt," Danny exclaimed. "And we could help you a lot, especially while you're down in bed and can't get out to look after things yourself."

"I know that," he went on. "But I want to think about it and pray about it tonight. Maybe I'll tell you what little I've found out in the morning."

"O.K.," Danny grinned.

"In the meantime keep your eyes and ears open," Mr. Blanshard said. "And if you see or hear anything, be sure and tell me all about it. It might be that you'll stumble onto the one thing that will solve the mystery."

Tip and Trixie's mother came in just then, and the kids said good-bye and scooted out.

"What do you make of it?" Tip whispered when they were out on the dock where no one from the house could hear them.

"I don't know," Danny said. "It gets more mysterious all the time. There are so many things here that just don't fit together. And yet it's got to go together somehow."

"I'd give plenty to know who that stranger at Penasse really is," Tip said, "and how he came to know so much about Dad getting hurt and everything. And why he warned Dad through you, not to go back to International Island and work on the cabin."

"And all the time the cabin had been burned," Trixie said.

"Why did he try to follow us?" Tip asked.

Danny Orlis picked up a dead minnow on the dock and tossed it to a gull that was circling overhead. The sharp-eyed bird swooped down and caught it with his bill in mid-air inches above the water.

"There's only one fellow up here who might know the answer to some of these things," Danny said, more to himself than to Tip and Trixie. "Old Rick Thunderbird knows just about everyone and everything that goes on in these parts."

Rick Thunderbird was an aged Indian friend of Danny's whom the young woodsman had been privileged to lead to the Lord. Rick seldom left his island, but he was a chief among his people, and somehow he managed to learn everything that was going on in the Angle.

"Do you suppose he'd tell us anything?" Tip asked.

"I think he would," Danny said, "if he happened to know anything about it. He's a very good friend of mine."

"Well, come on, then," Tip put in. "Let's go over and see Rick Thunderbird. What are we waiting for?"

As Danny swung the boat eastward out of Pine Creek and headed toward the Indian chief's island home just below Monument Bay, Trixie said, "What if that stranger sees us?"

"Say, now," her brother exclaimed, "that's a happy thought! You can just stop that kind of talk."

When they had ridden for ten or fifteen minutes Danny said, "You know, it was certainly wonderful to hear your dad say that he had taken Jesus as his personal Saviour."

"He didn't say that, did he?" Tip asked quickly.

"That's what he meant, anyway," Danny replied, "when he said that he had spent the morning in getting right with God."

Trixie had been sitting there quietly, acting as though she hadn't even heard what the boys were saying. Now she lifted her eyes and said, "I had the strangest feeling when I heard Daddy talk about getting right with God. For some reason I felt all dirty and unclean inside—just like I'd been wallowing in the mud and needed a bath; only it was where a bath wouldn't do any good."

"That's just the way we are before we let Jesus take over our lives," Danny told her. "We are dirty and unclean inside. Only it isn't mud we've been wallowing in. It's sin. That's why we have to turn to Jesus. His blood is the only thing that can wash the sin out of our lives."

Tip squirmed uncomfortably and began to toy with the tackle box as though it was the most important thing in the world right then.

Danny watched him carefully and prayed for words, prayed for the words that would tip the balances and make him turn to Jesus as his dad had done.

Trixie took off her wrist watch, wound it, and began to fumble with the band.

"Taking Jesus as your Saviour is the simplest thing in the world," Danny went on. "All you have to do is to confess the fact that you are a sinner and put your trust in Him to save you from the results of your sin. The big thing for you to do is to trust. The Lord will do the rest."

When Tip looked up a moment or two later he was biting his lower lip, and his mouth was set in a thin hard line.

"How far is it to this island where Rick Thunderbird lives?" he asked.

"We ought to be there in another five or ten minutes," Danny replied.

The young woodsman meant to go back to the subject immediately, but before he could do so Trixie began to chatter hurriedly about something or other, and the opportunity to talk to them more about the Lord Jesus Christ was gone.

Rick Thunderbird came hobbling out to meet the kids when they docked at his rocky little island.

"Danny," he said in his strange, broken English.

"You come to visit old Rick." He shook the young woodsman's hand with his thin, bony fingers. Danny introduced Tip and Trixie to him.

"This young man brought me the happiest day of my life," he said to them, "when he led me to Christ." They looked at one another strangely.

Rick, however, could not help very much with information about the stranger who had acted so strangely at Penasse.

"People come and go," he said. "Sometimes I hear about them. Sometimes no. Strangers there are in the Angle these days," he continued, his voice soft and musical. "Strangers who are not our kind of people. That much old Rick has learned. But why they are here—" He shrugged his shoulders expressively.

"You three come to big powwow with Rick. With ears and eyes open you learn something, maybe."

The disappointment showed on Danny's face.

"You say this man who followed you is Indian?" Rick asked.

"I'd say so," Danny replied. "And I know that he does-n't belong around here. I've never seen him before."

Rick Thunderbird shifted his gnarled cane to the other hand and leaned heavily upon it.

"We have a big powwow soon," he said. "Over on the Canadian mainland. All the Indians will be there. You three come with Rick. With ears and eyes open you learn something, maybe."

"But I thought your people wouldn't let white folks go to their powwows," Danny answered.

The old Indian drew himself up straight and tall. "Rick Thunderbird is still the Chief of his people," he said with authority. "If Rick takes you, you will be wel-comed as one of us."

"Boy, that's swell," Danny said.

On the way home Tip said, "I never knew an In-dian before. Isn't he a nice fellow?"

Danny told him, "I've got a lot of swell Indian friends. In all of us it's sin that causes the trouble. It isn't the fact that a man belongs to another race."

Trixie, who had been staring out over the horizon, half stood in the boat and cried, "Look!"

To the west of them, in an isolated section of the Minnesota shore the sky was suddenly a livid orange.

"Fire!" Danny exclaimed. "It's a forest fire!"

Chapter Eleven

THE SECOND FIRE

FOR TWO OR THREE SECONDS Tip, Trixie and Danny sat in the boat as though transfixed, staring at the brilliant orange flames that were dancing from the tops of the trees up toward the sky.

"Look!" Trixie exclaimed breathlessly. "There's a fire over there! The whole Angle's on fire!"

"I knew it was going to happen!" Danny gasped to himself. "I knew it was going to happen!"

"What are you going to do?" Tip asked excitedly.

"Go over there," Danny told him, heaving hard on the motor handle to send the boat around in a sweeping turn and head toward the blaze. "We're going to go over there and see what we can do about it!"

"We can't do anything about a fire like that," Tip protested. "It's got too big a start for us to even think of putting it out. We couldn't even begin to get close to it!"

"I never saw a fire spread so fast," Danny said, trying to coax a little more speed from the laboring motor.

"Neither have I," Trixie put in. "There wasn't any fire over there a minute or so ago."

"Look!" Trixie exclaimed breathlessly. "There's a fire over there! The whole Angle's on fire!"

"That's right," Danny went on. "It just burst into flame all at once, like there'd been a barrel of gasoline poured on things first."

"Do you suppose it was set too?" Tip asked. He shivered noticeably in spite of the warm afternoon sun. "Do you suppose someone set it afire?"

Danny was silent for a minute. "It must have been," he said finally. "We'll have to find out for sure."

"We aren't going over there now, are we, Danny?" Tip asked hesitantly. "The fellows who set it are probably still around there somewhere. We couldn't do anything by going over there now, could we, Danny?"

Danny didn't answer him for a moment or two.

"I don't know what we can do," he said. "But I want to take a good look at it."

His heart was beating a savage tattoo as the boat seemed to crawl over the water. A fire like that in the teeth of a strong wind could sweep across the muskeg as fast as a man could run, destroying everything in its path. And there would be little that anyone could do about it. It was strange, he thought, that the fire wasn't spreading rapidly already. The flames were leaping high in the air, and the smoke was billowing in great, choking clouds, but the fire didn't seem to be growing.

They had been some distance from the flames when they first saw it, but in five minutes or so the big motor had taken them close enough so they could see the shoreline clearly through the thick, billowing smoke.

"What do you know!" Danny exclaimed, cutting the motor's speed. "That fire isn't on the mainland at all!

The fire is on an island, and a small one at that!"

"Are you sure?" Trixie asked doubtfully. "It doesn't look like an island to me."

"It doesn't look like an island to me, either," her brother put in.

"It's an island just the same," the young woodsman told them. "I've been over here hundreds of times. The island that's afire is in the mouth of Riley Creek. We won't have to worry about it spreading. It never could leap the creek to get to the mainland."

Tip sighed in relief. "That's one good thing," he said fervently.

"But it's more mysterious than ever now," Danny told them. "Why would anyone set fire to the trees on a little island like this one if they wanted to burn out the Angle? That's what I can't figure out."

"Maybe whoever set it didn't want to burn out the Angle," Tip said. "Maybe they just wanted to burn the trees off the island for some reason."

"But why?" The young woodsman asked again. "What was there about the island that would make them want to burn it to destroy the trees? There isn't any good they could get out of it."

"And another thing," Trixie put in thoughtfully, "what sort of mystery could there be about that place on Harrison Creek where we put out that first forest fire the other day? No one's even lived back there for years and years."

"That," Danny replied tensely, "is the thing we've

got to find out." He turned the boat about and headed back toward his home on Pine Creek.

Danny was silent until they almost reached home. Then he said, "You know, I think we'd better take a little run back down toward Harrison Creek tomorrow morning, and then stop by Riley Creek on our way to the powwow in the afternoon. I think we ought to take a look at those places after the fires have burned out. Perhaps there's something we can find out by looking around over there."

"Oh, I don't know whether I'd dare to go back over there or not," Trixie shuddered. "It gives me goose pimples just to think of that man we saw watching us."

"Well, you could stay home if you'd want to," Danny said. "Tip and I would come back after you before we go over to the powwow."

"Nothing doing," she countered quickly. "If you're going over there I'm going to go too. You can't get away from me that easily."

The next morning as soon as breakfast and devotions were over Danny got busy with his chores, and by nine o'clock he was finished and ready to go over to Harrison Creek. He whistled sharply to Tip and Trixie to let them know that he was ready and filled his big motor with gasoline again.

"I thought Daddy was going to ask me about what we did yesterday," Trixie said when they were roaring over the placid water toward Harrison Creek. "But he was so busy reading the Bible that he didn't seem to be thinking about anything else. I don't believe he even knew when we got home."

"That's the way the Bible ought to be to all of us," Danny said. "I mean it ought to be so interesting that we just get lost reading it."

"But how can you get any fun out of reading one book all the time?" Tip asked. "I get so tired of just reading the same old stuff over and over that I can hardly stand it. I'd want something different, something with a little excitement in it."

"If it was just another book you'd probably be right, Danny explained."But it isn't just another book written by some men. If that's what it was it would have been forgotten a long while ago. But the Bible is God's Word. It's the way He chose to speak to us, the way He tells us how to be saved and how to live for Him."

Tip chewed on his lip and looked out across the brilliant blue water while Trixie sat there twisting her handkerchief into a tight little ball.

"Some people have the idea," Danny went on, "that the Bible is a book that's only for the teachers and ministers, but that's not right. It was written for everybody—even for you and me. It tells us how sin came into the world and how God sent Jesus to live on earth and die on the cross for our sins, and then to be raised again so that we can go to Heaven if we confess our sin and put our trust in Him to save us.''

"You don't have to preach all the time," Tip blurted angrily. "Don't you think I get tired of being preached to? Don't you think I get tired of stuff like that?"

Danny eyed him sharply and saw that his lower lip

was trembling. "Perhaps God is talking to you, Tip," he said softly, looking into his friend's wavering eyes. "Perhaps he's trying to plead with you to confess your sin and take the Lord Jesus Christ as your Saviour."

"I don't care if He is!" Tip cried. "I'm going to run my life the way I want to! I'm not going to be like you! All this praying, and not being able to do any of the things a fellow has fun doing! You make me sick!"

"You don't lose a thing when you take Christ as your Saviour, Tip," Danny went on. "You just substitute something far better for the old things you have been doing. Being a Christian is a wonderful, happy way to live!"

"You can sell that stuff to Trixie if you want to," Tip retorted. "That is if she's foolish enough to swallow it. But you can quit working on me. I'm going to live my own life!"

Silently Danny prayed that God would show Tip how heavy the burden of sin really is and that Christ offered the only way for him to be truly happy.

Chapter Twelve

TIMBER THIEVES

TIP BLANSHARD sat sullenly in the boat for half an hour or more until they turned into Harrison Creek and Danny cut the motor to half throttle.

"Keep your eye out for that place where we stopped the first time," the young woodsman said.

"Oh, we can't miss it," Trixie put in. "We're almost there now. I can recognize that big, gnarled pine tree."

Tip moved forward and croached on the deck of the big rowboat. "Head her in, Danny," he said. "I'll pull you up to shore." He jumped lightly to the bank as the boat eased up to the muskeg and pulled it up on shore a foot or so.

Trixie's eyes sparkled with excitement as she and Tip and Danny got out of the boat and went back into the forest.

"What do you suppose we'll find?" she asked, lowering her voice tensely.

"I don't have any idea," Danny told her. "Perhaps we won't find anything at all. But we'll soon know whether there's anything here that will help us to unravel part of this mystery."

For five or ten minutes they poked around the charred patch of timber, kicking the ashes with their feet and turning over the half-burned branches in which the fire had been put out before they were completely burned.

"Do you see anything?" Tip asked at last.

Danny shook his head.

"Neither do I!"

"The only thing I see," the young woodsman continued, "is that at some time or other this little patch of ground has been pretty well tramped over."

"Now how can you tell that?" Tip wanted to know. "It looks like any other deserted piece of woods to me."

Danny knelt beside a dead tree and picked up three or four broken branches. "Look at all the bent-over brush and broken twigs. That's a sure sign that there's been a lot of walking around here."

"Maybe we did it," Trixie put in. "We were running around here a lot the day of the fire, and we've been over it several times today."

"We probably did some of it," Danny admitted, "but not all of it. Some of these branches have been broken by someone who was pretty heavy: a lot heavier than we are." He sat down on a dead log. "I haven't seen a thing that looks as though it could have anything to do with the mystery, though," he said.

Trixie sighed and sat down on the other side of the log. "I've been hoping all the time that we'd find out something this morning," she said. "I was so excited I could hardly sleep last night."

Tip started to speak but Danny broke in excitedly, "Wait a minute!" he exclaimed, jumping to his feet. "What direction was the wind that day when we put out the fire here?"

"I don't know for sure," Tip said, "but it seems like it was in the northwest."

"That's the way I remember it too," Danny went on. "And if it was we've been looking in the wrong place all along."

"How do you figure that?" Trixie asked.

I just got to thinking," Danny said, "that if I was going to burn something in the woods I wouldn't set fire to the very spot where it was. I'd go up wind a little ways and build my fires so they could spread wider by the time they reached the things I wanted to burn,"

"If that's right," Tip continued, "then we'd ought to look over that way for whatever the fellow was trying to destroy."

"Well, come on," Trixie said, starting on ahead of them. "What are you waiting for?" By the time they had gotten to their feet she had disappeared into the brush ahead of them.

As Danny and Tip followed her they could hear her hurrying noisily on ahead of them.

"Have you found anything yet?" one of them called to her.

"Nope," she replied from somewhere just ahead. "I haven't found a thing but a bunch of stumps."

"Stumps!" Danny echoed. "Are you sure?"

"Of course I'm sure," she said, "don't you think I know what a stump looks like?"

"Stumps mean that there's been some timber cutting going on," Danny said as he and Tip hurried through the forest to where Trixie was standing. "And I don't know of any lumbering or pulp cutting that's been going on around here." Unless, and his heart sank at the thought of it, the paper company had already started to cut off the trees on the Angle.

In a moment or two they reached the spot where Trixie was standing.

"See," she said triumphantly. "Stumps. Just like I told you."

"See," she said triumphantly. "Stumps!
Just like I told you."

Danny looked at them in amazement. "These trees haven't been cut so very long," he said as though to himself. "And they're much too big for pulp wood. They were cut for lumber."

"But who'd be cutting timber way out here?' Tip asked. "And what could they do with it after they cut it?"

Danny sat down on a stump. "I just don't know," he said. "Has your dad said anything about the paper company doing any logging?"

"Nope," Trixie replied. "In fact he said that they were holding their timber up here in reserve and don't plan on doing any cutting on it for years and years."

While Trixie and Danny had been talking Tip had been walking about the cut-over stretch of forest. Now he came back to them and said, "If a thief or thieves wanted to steal some good pine trees for lumber, would there be any way of getting them out of here?"

"Sure," Danny said. "It would be a lot of work, but it could be done. All they would have to do would be to trim off the branches and tie the logs together. Then a boat could tow them out at night."

"But why would anyone go to all that trouble to get a few trees?" Trixie asked scornfully. "It looks to me like there are enough up here for everyone without stealing them."

"These aren't just ordinary trees," Danny explained. "They're pine, and pine lumber is worth an awful lot these days. A fellow could get rich stealing pine if he could get enough of it."

"That's just what I was thinking," Tip continued.

"Do you suppose that is what that stranger and the fellow Trixie saw spying on us that day we put out the forest fire here could be up to?"

Danny sat there for a long while. "I don't know," he said thoughtfully. "But it does make sense."

"What do you mean, makes sense?" Trixie asked impatiently. "I can't see that any of it makes sense. Why the forest fires? Why burn down our house? Why try to kill Dad?"

"Well," Danny replied, "they could have gotten scared when your dad came up here, if they were stealing timber off company property. That could account for their wanting to burn your cabin and cut the rungs on the ladder so he'd fall and get hurt. They might have been trying to scare him out."

"That's just the way I've got it figured," Tip went on. "And they could be setting these fires to burn over the land where they've done their cutting to destroy the stumps as evidence."

"That's it!" Danny exclaimed, jumping to his feet.

"That island in the mouth of Riley Creek had thirty-five or forty of the finest big pine trees you ever saw. I'll bet they cut them last winter, or most of them, and that's why they burned off the island!"

The kids looked at one another strangely as the full realization of what they uncovered came over them. "Then we are up against a gang of crooks!" Tip managed hoarsely.

Danny nodded. "And right dangerous crooks they can be, too, if we don't watch our step!"

Chapter Thirteen

A DESPERATE PLAN REVEALED

THAT VERY SAME AFTERNOON, as soon as dinner was over Trixie and Tip and Danny packed their tents and cooking gear into the boat and headed for Rick Thunderbird's and the Indian powwow.

"Do you suppose the thieves'll actually show up?" Trixie asked.

"Rick Thunderbird says that they will," Danny replied.

"What'll we do if we do see them or hear something?" she went on. "How're *we* going to be able to catch them?"

"Well," Danny said, "we'll just have to figure that out when we come to it."

Trixie shuddered.

"What's the matter?" Tip asked, joking. "Do you want to go back?"

"Don't be silly," she told him. "I wouldn't go back for anything."

The wind came up a little as they plowed among the islands, and here and there a large, billowing white cloud floated aimlessly by. For two or three minutes Tip sat there watching them. Then he said, "I've been hearing a lot about this powwow, but nobody's told me what it is."

"It's a sort of religious observance," Danny told him.

"It is!" Tip exclaimed in surprise. "I didn't know that that many Indians were Christian."

Danny shook his head. "They aren't," he said. "They're just as heathen as they were hundreds of years ago."

"Why, I didn't know that," Trixie put in.

"A lot of people don't," Danny said, "but most of them still have their sun dances and worship a piece of stone or a tree or a river. When you get sick they call on the local medicine man with his grand medicine bag, his pipe and his drum to use in chasing out the evil spirits."

"Oh, how awful!" she said.

"It's awful, all right," Danny agreed, "but the Indians don't know any better. Most of them worship the things that they do because they've never heard of the Lord Jesus who died on the cross and rose again so they could have eternal life." He stopped a moment to adjust the motor. "Think how much worse it must seem to God," he went on, "for those who live down in the States where they hear the Gospel on every corner, where ministers and friends have talked to them about taking Jesus as their personal Saviour and they still haven't done it."

Trixie's face whitened, and her lips drew down to a thin, hard line. Quickly she dropped her head. Tip looked grimly out across the water, while Danny sat there and prayed. Finally Danny said softly, "Trixie, wouldn't you like to take Jesus as your personal Saviour?"

She raised her head and nodded. A tear sneaked out from under her eyelid and trickled slowly down her cheek.

"Why don't you just bow your head," Danny suggested softly, "and pray that God will be merciful unto you and forgive your sins?"

"Is that all there is to it?" Trixie asked.

"That's all there is to it," Danny said. "If you confess the fact that you are a sinner who needs saving and put your trust in Jesus to save you, then you're a Christian."

She hesitated a moment. "But what if I can't live up to it?" she asked seriously.

"If you had to trust in yourself that would be a real problem," Danny told her, "but you don't. And neither do I, nor does anyone else. We can put our trust in Jesus to keep us walking the way we should."

For a brief instant Trixie sat there staring straight ahead. Then she dropped carefully to her knees on the bottom of the boat and began to pray. Danny didn't know whether she prayed silently or aloud, for he couldn't hear her above the roar of the motor. But when she finally raised her head and got back on the seat her face was radiant. For a long while she just sat there smiling. Then she said, "You'll never know how hard I fought to keep from taking Jesus as my Saviour. I felt that it would be the end of my good times and everything else. Now I know how Dad felt when—"

"Shut up, will you?" Tip exclaimed angrily. "I'm getting sick and tired of it."

"I felt the same way, Tip," Trixie replied, "until a few minutes ago."

"I don't care if you did," he said; "just leave me alone!"

At the powwow Rick introduced Danny and Tip and Trixie to the other Indian leaders. "These are my friends," he said.

For an hour or so Danny and his companions walked slowly around the grounds. The dances were already in progress to the accompaniment of weird rhythm of the tom-toms and the strange singing monotone of the dancers.

"Did you ever see anything like this before?" Tip whispered to Danny.

"Yes," he nodded, "but I don't know just what dance this is."

The Indians who were looking on were dressed as most white people do, only a little poorer, but the dancers were in all of their ancient Indian finery. The women wore fawn-colored buckskin dresses that were fringed and weighted with beautiful beaded designs. "The men wore buckskin too, with feathered head dresses and sparkling moccasins. Trixie gasped when she saw them.

"It just makes my heart ache to watch them," she said after a time. "To think that they live up here and worship idols and die without a chance to learn of Jesus. Aren't there any missionaries here, Danny?"

"Not very many," he said. "At least none of them ever get up here where it's really wild."

"It just makes me feel like I'd ought to be a missionary to them," she said.

They watched for several minutes. The dance seemed to be without beginning or end as the Indians bobbed up and down in rhythm to their drums and singing in that haunting, unmusical tone.

"Let's go over where they're cooking their supper," Tip whispered at last, touching Danny on the shoulder.

Off in one corner of the big clearing some thirty or forty Indian women were squatting about eight or ten big iron kettles working and talking busily. Earlier in the afternoon the kettles had been filled with water and fires started under them. Now the water was boiling and little wisps of steam were curling up to mingle with thc smoke. The women were cutting up pieces of meat and tossing them into the kettles. And, every now and then one of them would get up and stir the water with a big stick, or scoop up a piece of meat, bite off a piece and throw the rest back into the kettle.

"What are they doing?" Tip whispered to Danny.

"Oh, they're cutting up deer meat and making stew," he said. "Everybody eats together at a powwow."

"Well, I'm not going to eat with them," Tip announced firmly.

They had almost circled the clearing and were approaching the dancers again when Trixie chanced to look around. There, not twenty feet from her, stood a man with bushy dark hair and piercing eyes and a scowl on his face. She stopped suddenly and grasped Danny by the arm, squeezing it hard!

"That's him!" she whispered. "That's him!"

The man turned as she spoke and stared at them. Danny would have sworn that his face whitened.

Then he turned on his heel and went striding through the crowd.

"That was him!" Trixie said, staring after the stranger. "That was the fellow I saw peeking over the brush at us that day of the first forest fire!"

"Are you sure?" Danny asked excitedly.

"Of course I'm sure," she replied. "I'd know that face anywhere!"

"Are you positive that was the guy?" Tip put in.

"I'm as positive of it as I am that I'm talking to you," Trixie said. "That day of the fire those eyes just looked right through me and gave me the cold chills. And I felt the same way today. I know that's the man!"

Tip was chewing his tongue and looking hurriedly over the crowd as though he half expected them all to turn and come charging after him. He tried hard to act as though he wasn't scared, but he wasn't fooling anybody. "Now what're we going to do?" he asked.

Danny thought for a moment or two. "The first thing we ought to do is to see whether he's alone or if the other strange Indian or somebody else is here with him," he said.

"The worst of it is," Tip went on, "he knows that we're here and that we recognized him!"

Danny nodded. "He and whoever else is with him is warned now," he said, looking out over the milling crowd. "I think the best thing we can do is locate him again and tail him until we find out whether or not he is alone."

"But what if he sees us?" Tip asked quickly.

"It'll be our job to keep him from seeing us," Danny replied.

Supper was over, and it was almost dark when they finally caught a glimpse of the mysterious stranger again. He was standing on the fringe of the crowd talking rapidly with the man who was beside him. Danny touched Tip's rib with his finger and motioned for him and Trixie to slip off to one side.

"That's him," Trixie said.

"But who's that man with him?" Tip asked.

Danny edged slowly forward until he could see the other man's face. "It's just as I thought," he whispered when he came back to where Tip and Trixie were. standing. "It's the strange Indian! I thought the two of them were linked together somehow."

While the kids stood there whispering, the two men began to move away from the crowd.

"Let's slip over there behind that bunch of trees," Danny said, "and see if we can get closer to them, close enough to hear what they're saying."

With the trees and darkness to screen them it wasn't too difficult.

"I thought I'd never find you," the one Trixie had first seen said softly. "I've been hunting for you for an hour."

"I'd feel better if we went back to our tent to do our talking, Mac," the strange Indian grumbled. "Somebody's going to hear us out here."

"Nobody's paying any attention to us, Joe," the other said. "They don't even know we're around. It's those kids we've got to worry about."

"Are you sure they recognized you?" Joe asked.

"Of course I'm sure," his companion replied.

"Do you suppose they know anything?" Joe persisted.

"That's the big question," Mac said. "I did find out that old Rick Thunderbird brought them out here. Guess old Rick took a fancy to that Orlis brat."

"Those're the Blanshard kids that are with young Orlis," Joe went on. "I saw them together over at Penasse."

"That's right," Mac said. "And there's a chance that they know more than we think they do. We'll have to get on with things, fast."

"Now you're talkin'." Joe stepped a bit closer to his companion and lowered his voice until they could scarcely hear what he was saying. "We'll slip out before dawn tomorrow," he went on, "and be back

"*They don't even know we're around. It's those kids we've got to worry about.*"

here before anybody even misses us."

"That sounds O.K. to me," Mac said. "We'd better get over to Bear River and take care of that first; and then go over to Harrison Creek. I'll meet you down in the bay at 3:30."

They checked their watches to see that they both had the same time. Then one of them strolled casually off, and the other rejoined the group that was watching the dancers.

The kids stood behind the trees until the men were gone. Then Danny touched Trixie and Tip on the arm and drew them back into the trees another ten or fifteen yards.

"What do you make of that?" Tip asked, his voice tense.

"Joe and Mac are the ones who've been stealing the pines for lumber," Danny said. "That much is sure."

"But why would they want to start fires now?" Trixie asked. "What's the use of destroying trees they haven't taken?"

"The way I've got it figured," Danny continued, "is that they've been trying to make things so rough on your dad that he'd move out and to cover up their thefts at the same time. If they can scare him away before he finds out about the stealing that's going on, they probably think that the company won't be the wiser, and they can go on and on with their cutting of L & R land."

"And now they're going to start a couple of other fires," Tip added in a hoarse whisper, "at Bear River and Harrison Creek!"

Chapter Fourteen

HIDDEN TRAPS

"WHAT'RE WE GOING TO DO?" Trixie asked, her fingers quivering with excitement and her forehead beaded with sweat, "Go back and tell Dad?"

"What could he do about it?" Tip cut in. "He wouldn't even be able to get out of bed if he were here. It wouldn't do any good to tell Dad."

"Maybe we could get your dad, Danny," Trixie said hopefully. "He'd come over here with us, wouldn't he?"

"He isn't home," Danny replied. "He had to go over to Oak Island this afternoon, and he won't be back until sometime tomorrow."

"I know," Tip said eagerly. "We could go get the Mounties. We could tell them what we've found out and let them go stop Mac and Joe from setting the fires."

"We'd have to go up to Kenora to get them, Tip," Danny said. "We could never do that and get back before they got the fires set and going good. And besides, if there'd happen to be a strong wind tomorrow, half the Angle could be afire before we could do anything about it."

"But we can't just stay here and let them get away with it," Tip said emphatically. "We've got to do something!"

For several minutes they stood there in silence, looking at one another. Then Danny said, "I don't suppose it'd do any good to tell Rick Thunderbird. He's so crippled with rheumatism that he wouldn't be able to help us. And we don't know anybody else here that we could ask for help."

"And," Trixie said awkwardly, "it wouldn't do any good for us to go over there, would it?"

"I was just wondering that myself," Danny said slowly.

"You—you mean for us to—to go over there," Tip stammered, "right over there w-w-where those fellows are going?"

Danny nodded.

"But what could we do?" Tip asked, his voice trembling. "We don't have a gun or anything."

"We could make a lot of noise and scare them away," Danny said, "or we could slip up and take their canoe and leave them stranded. They wouldn't dare to set a fire unless they had a way of getting out of there."

"But that wouldn't be right, would it?" Trixie asked; "taking their canoe would be dishonest."

"Oh, we wouldn't take it with the idea of keeping it," Danny replied. "We'd just take it to trap them over there at Bear River and keep them from setting another forest fire."

"I'm not worried about that," Tip put in quickly. "What's got me scared is getting in the canoe in the first place. What would we do if those guys catch us?"

"We'll just have to pray," Trixie said. "We'll have to put our trust in God to keep them from catching us."

Tip stared at her but said nothing.

"We'd better get back to our tents and get some heavier jackets and something to eat," Danny said softly, "and then get over to Bear River."

"You mean we ought to start out now?" Tip asked.

"We'll have to if we're going to be there before Mac and Joe get there," Danny replied. "We'll all meet at the boat in ten minutes."

It was dark now, so dark that Danny could scarcely make out the winding forest trail to the place where their boat was beached. Carefully he inched along the path, thankful for the strumming tom-toms and the drone of Indian voices that drowned out the sound of his steps. Somehow, as he crept stealthily forward an uneasy feeling came over him, as though someone was following his every move.

"O God," he prayed silently, "just be with us and help us. In Jesus' name."

Finally he reached the boat and squatted breathlessly beside it to wait for Trixie and Tip.

"Is—is that you, Tip?" he whispered as a shadowy form approached him.

"Yeh," Tip replied. "Is Trixie here yet?"

Neither Danny nor Tip had heard her come up, but

now she said softly, and almost in her brother's ears, "I'm right behind you."

At the sound of her voice Tip jumped as though he'd stepped on a rattlesnake, and he stifled a sputtering little yell.

Trixie laughed musically. "What's the matter?" she asked. "Did I scare you?"

"Who—me?" he echoed.

Danny had already untied the anchor rope from about the tree and was pushing the boat out into the lake. "Come on," he said softly. "We can't risk the noise of the motor so we've got a lot of rowing to do tonight."

Silently he slipped the oars into the locks and began to row, with long, rhythmic strokes that sent the boat gliding noiselessly through the water.

"D-d-don't you think we ought to go back?" Tip asked. "If those guys catch us it'll be the end of us."

"But they aren't going to catch us," Trixie said quickly.

"I don't mind telling you," Tip went on, "I'm scared."

"You know, Tip," Danny said evenly. "There are times when a fellow just has to do something and put his trust in God to watch over him and care for him while he does it. This is one of those times."

"That's all right for you and Trixie," Tip said. "You can say that, but I can't." He was silent for a long while. "I haven't put my trust in Jesus," he almost whispered.

Danny stopped rowing now and leaned on his oars. "Maybe you haven't yet, Tip," he said quietly. "But you can. All you have to do is to confess your sins and put your trust in Jesus, believing that He's got the power to save you from the consequences of those sins. It's as simple as that."

"I—I've been doing a lot of thinking about it," he said hoarsely. "Some nights I guess I haven't even been able to sleep very much because of it. I always thought I lived a good enough life for anybody until you began to quote some of the Bible to me."

"The Bible's got a way of doing that to us," Danny said. "It shows us just how bad and wrong some of the things we do really are."

"But I—I just couldn't give up all the good times and everything," Tip continued. "It costs too much to be a Christian."

Although Danny couldn't see Trixie's face he knew that, while he talked with Tip, she was busy praying.

"A lot of people say that it costs too much to be a Christian," Danny said. "But just think what it costs not to be a Christian. It costs you all the real happiness a Christian has while he's here on earth. It costs you all the joy of Heaven. It costs you an eternity in Hell, separated from God and your loved ones who've taken Jesus as their personal Saviour. Maybe it does seem to somebody who isn't a Christian like it costs an awful lot to be one. But the way I look at it, it costs a lot more not to be."

"I—I hadn't thought of that," Tip said lamely.

Danny sat there, waiting and praying.

"I thought it cost a lot to be a Christian," Trixie put in prayerfully, "but I found out that it really doesn't. After you've become a Christian those things you give up don't mean anything to you at all. I think that the idea of it costing so much to be a Christian is just one of the Devil's tricks to keep us from Jesus."

"Would—would you help me, Danny?" Tip asked at last. "Would you help me take Jesus as my personal Saviour too?"

"Sure I will, Tip," Danny said, his heart singing. Quietly he put the oars away, and there, halfway across the stretch of water between the Canadian mainland and Bear River, in the middle of the night, Danny Orlis began to explain the way of salvation to Tip. And when at last they bowed their heads to pray, Trixie knelt quietly in the prow of the boat to thank God that her brother had found Jesus.

The boat was hard to row. The first faint streaks of dawn began to chase the darkness away when Danny and Tip and Trixie pulled into the mouth of the Bear River.

"If I remember right," Danny said, "the pine trees here used to be on the west bank; right along there."

Tip stood in the boat and peered intently into the trees. "I think I see some stumps up ahead," he said.

In a moment or two Trixie confirmed it. "Oh, there's a lot of them," she said. "It looks like a regular clearing."

Danny nodded, more to himself than his companions. "Then, if I've got it figured out right they'll start their fires over there some place." Quickly he swung the boat about.

"What're you going to do?" Tip wanted to know.

"Get this boat out of sight," Danny said quickly. "Mac and Joe'll be along here any minute."

As Danny began to row back toward the Lake of the Woods he noted for the first time that dark, rolling clouds were churning over the horizon, and the wind which had been at their backs during the night had switched abruptly.

"Boy, we've got to get them stopped before they get a fire going today," Danny said. "With a wind like this it'd spread a mile a minute."

A hundred yards or so back toward the lake he came upon a little cove with brush hanging out over the water to form a perfect hiding place for their craft. Danny angled into it, and in a couple of minutes they had the boat so well concealed that a stranger could walk within a dozen feet of it and never know it was there.

"Now to get ourselves hid," Tip said, "before Mac and Joe get here."

"Say," Danny exclaimed, stopping short. "I just thought of something! Dad and I set some bear traps out here last winter and never did pick them up. Whatever you do, watch your step."

"Bear traps?" Tip echoed. "What'd happen if we stepped on one?"

"It'd almost cut your leg off," Danny said.

While the two boys had been talking Trixie had been looking out over the lake. Now she touched Danny on the arm and whispered, "Here they come."

Sure enough, a long, lithe Indian canoe was knifing through the water toward them, two men bending hard over the paddles. There was no question about it! It was Mac and Joe!

"Come on," Danny said, "we've got to get down, quick." Hurriedly he guided Tip and Trixie to a secluded patch of brush where they could see without being seen. "Now we'll see where they leave their canoe," he whispered.

While they waited tensely for the two men to reach the river each one whispered a prayer. "I—I don't know much about praying," Tip said uncertainly, "But, O God, help us to stop them before they set the whole forest afire."

For several minutes they lay there waiting. Then suddenly they began to hear the sound of voices. Danny raised up cautiously and peeked out. "Oh no," he said, "we guessed too close to where they were coming. They've stopped within a hundred yards of our boat."

"W-w-what're we going to do?" Tip asked.

"There isn't anything we can do now," Danny said.

"Come on," Joe was saying impatiently. "Let's get this job over with and get out of here."

"Take it easy a minute, will you?" Mac asked.

Joe was already walking noisily through the trees. "We probably wouldn't have needed this gasoline," he said.

There was no chance for Danny and his friends to get to the canoe. Somehow Mac had managed to stay between it and them.

"Are you all set?" he called to Joe who'd gone ahead some seventy-five or a hundred yards.

"All set," Joe answered. Then they heard the crackle of flames followed by Joe's low chuckle. "I guess this ends the evidence," he said.

"Well, come on," Mac called to him irritably.

Although Danny hadn't noticed, the wind had gone down during the time Mac and Joe landed on the bank of the river and made their way back into the woods. Now it switched quickly and came up with a roar.

"The wind!" the kids heard Mac cry. "We've got to get out of here!"

"Let's get going!" Danny said between clenched teeth.

"But they'll see us!" Tip protested.

"We've got something worse than that to worry about!" Danny said. "That fire's going to be blown back on us any minute!"

Hurriedly they ran for their boat. As they reached it they saw Mac run down to the canoe, throw it into the water and leap into it. At that very moment they heard a scream of terror from somewhere behind them.

"Mac! Mac!" Joe screamed. "I'm in a trap! I'll burn

"Mac! Mac!" Joe screamed. "I'm in a trap! I'll burn up! Mac! Come back for me! Mac!"

up! Mac! Come back for me! Mac!"

Danny froze where he was standing, and the color drained from his face. Joe had stumbled into one of those bear traps, and the fire was roaring down upon him!

Chapter Fifteen

A THIEF REPENTS

DANNY, TRIXIE AND TIP stood there, rooted to the ground, the smoke burning their nostrils and smarting their eyes as they stared at one another, and at Mac who was paddling wildly out into the big lake. Another long, agonizing scream of terror shrilled above the wind and crackling flames.

"Did you hear that?" Danny asked, his mouth suddenly gone dry with fear.

And then the cry came again. "Mac! I can't get loose!" the voice cried in terror. "Come back after me, Mac! Mac! Mac!"

"He's in one of our bear traps," Danny exclaimed. "I've got to go back after him!"

"But you can't," Trixie protested. "You'll be killed!"

"If I don't," Danny said quickly, "Joe'll be killed."

Quickly he took his handkerchief from his pocket, dipped it in the water, and tied it about his nose and mouth.

"Well, if you're going," Tip said, "I'm going with you."

"And so am I," Trixie said.

"No, Trixie," Danny told her. "You can do more good by getting the boat out into the river and keeping it there where there's no chance of the fire getting at it until we get back."

She started to argue with him, then stopped quickly and said, "Anyway, I'll be praying for both of you."

"Swell," Danny and Tip said almost together; and then they turned and began to make their way into the woods.

The wind was still raging high, blowing the flames before it and fanning the sparks that blew ahead from tree to tree. There was no time to stop to kneel and pray, but Danny and Tip prayed with every burning gasp of breath, with every step into the woods. All Danny could think of was the man who would be burned to death unless he and Tip got there in time.

"O God!" he prayed, "give us the strength to get to him before the fire does. Help us, O Lord, to get Joe out alive and well!"

"Do you think we'll make it?" Tip choked as they paused a moment, fighting for breath.

"We'll make it," Danny said determinedly. "We've got to make it!"

Joe's screams for Mac guided them toward him, though they were coming now in long, hacking gasps.

"Here," Danny said as he reached him and seized him by the arm. "We've got to get you out of here."

"Where's Mac?" Joe exclaimed hoarsely.

"He couldn't wait for you," Tip said simply.

It was all that the two boys could do to open the ugly jaws wide enough so Joe could pull his torn and bleeding leg out of it.

"Mac ran off and left me?" he asked dazedly. "I can't understand it."

Even as he talked Tip and Danny went to work. The trap was old and rusty but the springs were powerful, and it was all that the two boys could do to open the ugly jaws wide enough so Joe could pull his torn and bleeding leg out of it. The gashes were long and ragged, and his trousers' leg was soaked with blood.

"This smoke's getting thicker and thicker," Danny said, choking and gasping as he spoke. "Do you think you can walk, Joe?"

The injured man winced in pain as he put his foot to the ground.

"Here," Danny ordered. "Tip and I'll help you." Obediently Joe put a heavy arm about each boy's shoulder and began to hobble toward the river.

The smoke was getting thicker every moment, but going away from the fire didn't seem to make the heat feel so intense, and in a matter of minutes the three of them reached the river where Trixie was standing by with the boat.

"Oh, thank God!" she breathed reverently as she saw them. "Thank God!"

Quickly the boys got Joe into the boat and shoved away.

The Indian's face was white and drawn with pain, and his breath was coming in long sobs. Beads of sweat stood out on his forehead, and his hands were trembling.

"Tip," Danny said as he started the motor and swung the boat about to head toward Angle Inlet, "can you and Trixie take that first-aid kit and stop the bleeding?"

"Sure thing," Tip said. Quickly he cut away the injured man's trousers' leg and put the tourniquet in place above the knee while Trixie washed out the deep, jagged cuts with a strong disinfectant.

"We'll have to have him flown out to Rosseau or Warroad," Danny said softly.

"I'll be all right," Joe muttered. "Just get me to my cabin."

"We'll see what the doctor's got to say first," Danny said.

"But what about the fire?" Tip broke in.

"We've got to get Joe taken care of first," Trixie said.

Danny nodded his agreement. The motor had seemed to push the boat so fast before, but now it seemed to crawl over the choppy, foam-laced waves. He looked down at the pain-twisted face of Joe and then away. Wouldn't they ever get to Angle Inlet?

For several minutes no one spoke. And then Danny saw a plane appear just above the trees in the direction of Oak Island and head straight as an arrow for the Bear River.

"Look!" he said, pointing toward the plane. "There's our answer to the fire. I don't know why I didn't think of that before. Somebody saw the smoke and is going up to investigate. It won't be long until they'll have a couple of dozen men flown in to fight it."

"Yes," Tip said, "but the fire's apt to be out of control by the time they get there."

"If they can get to it before the wind changes, they'll be all right," Danny said. "It's blowing straight toward the lake now, and there's only a little patch of a hundred acres or so in that triangle between the lake and the river and the place where Joe and Mac started the fire."

"That's right," Trixie put in, smiling for the first time in hours. "It seems strange," she went on, as much to herself as the others, "but I've been praying that God would help us to get the forest fire put out. Then when we had to get Joe and rush him to a doctor without doing anything at all about the fire I got to thinking that maybe God wasn't going to answer our prayers after all. But just look. He's sending men who can do so much more than we could in getting the fire out."

"That's the way it is with prayer," Danny told her. "We pray for something and then expect God to answer our prayer in a certain way. When He doesn't do it just like we think He should, we get the idea it isn't going to be answered at all. But His answer is always so much better than the one that we've worked out."

Joe groaned a little and Trixie and Tip both knelt beside him. His lips moved slowly, but he did not speak. In a moment or two Tip inched back to Danny and whispered in his ear, "Joe's pulse is getting awfully fast and weak. Can't you get any more speed out of this crate?"

Danny shook his head. The minutes crawled slowly by, one by one. It might be that Carl Orlis and all the other men in the area would be up on the Bear River fighting the forest fire. Maybe there wouldn't be anyone at Angle Inlet to get Joe down to a doctor. If there wasn't anyone to help him, Joe might—Danny could not even bring himself to think about it. With every wave and every throb of the motor he prayed for the injured man who lay in the boat at his feet.

"Tip," he said, "you'd better loosen that tourniquet for a couple of minutes so we don't destroy the circulation in his leg."

Joe didn't move as Tip worked over him, and seemed to be asleep as they turned in at the creek and roared up to the Orlis' dock.

Carl Orlis and half a dozen grim-faced settlers were waiting there for the plane to take them to the Bear River.

As the boat came slamming up to the dock Danny yelled, "Dad! Come here, quick! We've got a fellow who's awful bad hurt!"

Mr. Orlis took a quick look at Joe as the others crowded about. "I'll say you have," he said. "We'll get some hot water bottles and wrap him up good to keep him warm and leave him right in the boat until Eddie gets back with the *Sea Bee*. We'll have Ed fly him down to the hospital in Rosseau."

"Say," one of the men said. "I know this fellow. He's

Joe McCarran, a buddy of that ex-convict Mac Duval and a bad actor if I ever saw one."

"That's the other one!" Trixie exclaimed. "He called the other fellow Mac!"

"What do you mean, young lady?" Mr. Orlis asked. "How did you kids get mixed up with these men, anyway?"

Quickly Danny and Tip and Trixie told the whole story, how they had put out the first forest fire and had been followed from Penasse by Joe, and how they'd seen the two of them over at the Indian powwow and had heard them plan to set another fire at Bear River and Harrison Creek.

"And then," Danny concluded, "when we heard Joe scream that he'd been caught in one of our bear traps, Tip and I went back and got him and brought him here."

Mr. Orlis whistled in surprise. "All this going on under our very noses," he said, "and we didn't know what was happening."

"We should've known there was something fishy about those fires," one of the others said. "We go along for years and don't have any fires to speak of, and then in a week we have three. We should've known there was something behind them."

Ed came winging in with his *Sea Bee* just then and Danny, Tip and Trixie helped to load the injured Joe into the cabin of the plane.

"And, Ed," Carl Orlis said hoarsely, "get hold of the sheriff down there and have him place this fellow under arrest. He's going to have a lot to answer for when he gets out of the hospital."

"O.K.."

"And," Mr. Orlis went on, "tell him to make out a warrant for Mac Duval and send a deputy up here right away, or deputize you. We're going to get that fellow, and anyone else who's involved in this thing before they slip through our fingers."

The kids watched until the sturdy *Sea Bee* was airborne and speeding toward Rosseau, and then they turned and went into the Blanshard cabin. Mr. Blanshard was sitting in a big chair near the window, his head still heavily bandaged.

"Well, now," he said when they told him the story, "that is something. I don't tell you what I've found out because I'm afraid you'll poke around and get hurt, and you go ahead and solve the mystery and find the guilty men besides."

"The Lord had an awful lot to do with it," Tip said. His dad eyed him a moment or two and then said, "Yes, Tip, I'm sure that He did."

"There's one thing I've been wondering about, Mr. Blanshard," Danny said slowly.

"And what's that?" the man asked.

"Well, when you first came up here," he began, "the story got out that the paper company was going to bring in a force of men and cut down all the timber on the Angle. A lot of us were sure worried."

Mr. Blanshard shook his head. "No," he said, "we

haven't got anything like that in mind. That story must've been started by Mac and Joe and the others in the deal. I'm a special operative for the L & R. We got wind that there was illegal cutting taking place on our land here so the company sent me to find out about it. I didn't know you kids were going to make the job so easy."

The three of them looked at him and grinned.

"I think," he went on, "that I'm going to ask to be stationed here permanently. Would you like that?"

"I'll say we would," Trixie and Tip said together.

It was the next day that Joe McCarran sent word with Eddie that he wanted to see Danny and Tip and Trixie.

"And I've got to go back this afternoon," Ed said, "so if you want to hop in you can go along."

When they filed in to Joe's room he grinned feebly at them. "I guess I really owe you kids a lot," he said.

"We were sure glad we were around so we could help you," Danny told him.

"And that's another thing I can't figure out," Joe went on. "Here, me and Mac did everything we could against you and—and then you risked your lives to save me. How come?"

"Well," Trixie said, "we couldn't leave you out there to die. And besides we knew that you did the things you were doing because you don't know Jesus as your personal Saviour."

Danny thought he could see Joe's lips quiver. For

three full minutes they stood there waiting for him to speak. When he did his eyes were soft and some of the hardness was gone out of his mouth. "If being a Christian will make you kids like you are," he said softly, "it's something I need. Tell me about this Jesus, will you please?"

Danny and Tip and Trixie were smiling as they moved close to Joe's bed and began to read to him out of Danny's pocket Testament.

For a complete list of available books, write to:
Sword of the Lord Publishers
P. O. Box 1099
Murfreesboro, Tennessee 37133.

(800) 251-4100
(615) 893-6700
FAX (615) 848-6943
www.swordofthelord.com